Destinations 1
Grammar for Academic Success

Nancy Herzfeld-Pipkin
GROSSMONT COLLEGE

HEINLE
CENGAGE Learning™

Australia • Brazil • Japan • Korea • Mexico • Singapore • Spain • United Kingdom • United States

HEINLE
CENGAGE Learning™

Destinations 1:
Grammar for Academic Success
Nancy Herzfeld-Pipkin

Publisher: Sherrise Roehr

Acquisitions Editor: Tom Jefferies

Assistant Editor: Lauren Stephenson

Director of Content and Media Production:
Michael Burggren

Marketing Director, U.S.:
Jim McDonough

Director of Adult Education Sales:
Eric Bredenberg

Marketing Communications Manager:
Beth Leonard

Sr. Product Marketing Manager:
Katie Kelley

Sr. Content Product Manager:
Maryellen Eschmann-Killeen

Sr. Print Buyer: Mary Beth Hennebury

Development Editor: Sarah Barnicle

Compositor: Parkwood Composition
Services

Cover Designer: Gina Petti/Rotunda Design
House

Credits appear on page vi, which
constitutes a continuation of the
copyright page.

For product information and technology assistance, contact us at
Cengage Learning Academic Resource Center, 1-800-423-0563

For permission to use material from this text or product, submit all
requests online at **cengage.com/permissions**
Further permission questions can be emailed to
permissionrequest@cengage.com

Library of Congress Control Number: 2009932080
ISBN 10: 1-4130-2244-8
ISBN 13: 978-1-4130-2244-5

Heinle, Cengage Learning
20 Channel Center Street
Boston, MA 02210
USA

Cengage Learning is a leading provider of customized learning
solutions with office locations around the globe, including
Singapore, the United Kingdom, Australia, Mexico, Brazil and
Japan. Locate our local office at:
international.cengage.com/region

Cengage Learning products are represented in Canada by
Nelson Education, Ltd.

Visit Heinle online at **elt.heinle.com**
Visit our corporate website at **cengage.com**

Printed in Canada.
1 2 3 4 5 6 7 — 13 12 11 10 09

To *the* Teacher

Destinations 1: Grammar for Academic Success was written to provide students a full range of grammar practice at the high intermediate level. By incorporating unit themes, contexts, and vocabulary from its companion book *Destinations 1: Writing for Academic Success,* the *Destinations* grammar workbook is designed to be used as a supplementary text in writing courses or as the grammar text in linked writing and grammar courses.

LINKS TO *DESTINATIONS 1: WRITING FOR ACADEMIC SUCCESS*

- Grammar points covered in each unit will be especially useful in student writing assignments of the writing text. Grammar topics were chosen with the writing assignments in mind.
- Examples of sentence patterns and sentence combining techniques taught in the writing book also appear in the corresponding units of the grammar workbook.
- Vocabulary from the writing book is recycled in the grammar lessons of the corresponding units.
- The materials in the grammar workbook closely follow the order of the same thematic material introduced in the writing book. That is, the grammar points at the beginning of a unit follow the information or topics presented at the beginning of the corresponding writing unit. In the same way, the topics that are presented at the end of the writing book unit are presented at the end of the grammar book unit as well.
- Some exercises and activities expound on the topics introduced in the writing book. Other topics may be somewhat different from information presented in the writing book, but they are always closely related.

OVERVIEW OF UNITS

Each of the six units in the grammar workbook corresponds to a unit in the *Destinations 1* writing text. Each grammar unit contains five to eight lessons; each of the 37 lessons covers one grammar point or sometimes two related grammar points. In addition, in Unit Four the topic of modals is introduced with general information.

OVERVIEW OF LESSONS

- Each lesson provides a variety of activities/exercises in order to afford students many opportunities to practice and participate. Due to the variations in time and purpose of individual classes, it is not necessarily expected that every teacher will cover everything in each lesson. Teachers should feel free to choose those activities that best suit the needs and abilities of their particular students.
- Many of the exercises in this book have more than one possible answer.
  1. In some of the more structured activities, the directions explicitly tell students that more than one answer may be appropriate.
  2. In the less structured exercises many answers are possible. These exercises have been included to show students that several variations may be acceptable. It is hoped this approach will help them when dealing with English outside the classroom where they may encounter such variations. It is also hoped that this approach will help students comfortably use and manipulate the language.

PRESENTATION OF LESSONS

Each lesson presents a grammar topic and provides practice with the grammar in the following ways:

1. *Photo or illustration with example sentences*
   The photo or illustration reviews or relates to a topic in the *Destinations* writing text. The accompanying example sentences introduce the grammar and often include recycled vocabulary or ideas from the writing text.
2. *Questions*
   The questions ask students to focus on the grammar of the lesson by analyzing specific parts of the example sentences. This section is meant as an inductive exercise for students to figure out (or state as review) the grammar point.
3. *Explanation*
   This section provides rules, charts, and discussion of the grammatical focus of the lesson. This is the only part of the lesson that does not ask students to complete a task.
4. *Practice*
   Each lesson begins with controlled exercises. These exercises ask students to fill in the blanks, complete matching activities, answer true or false questions about given sentences, or choose the correct form. Every lesson also presents an error correction or editing exercise that asks students to find the mistakes and correct them.

   Each lesson also has some activities that ask students to be more creative and independent. In all of these activities, students must use the particular grammatical structure from the lesson as much as possible. Some activities ask students to complete sentences using given words or information. Others ask students to create their own sentences based on specific situations or information. These activities often afford students an opportunity to write about topics related to those they may write about for assignments in the *Destinations 1* writing text.

Although all the exercises in the text can be used as pair or group work, the exercises that would work especially well in groups are marked with the group icon, which is also found in the writing text. Many exercise directions make suggestions for pair work and class work.

Marked by this icon, references to *Destinations 1: Writing for Academic Success* have been made throughout the grammar text's explanations and exercises. There are numerous suggestions for review of topics such as sentence patterns as well as use of transitions and coordinating and subordinating conjunctions. The writing examples students encounter in the grammar workbook will reinforce many of the concepts learned in the writing text.

APPENDICES

The appendices include reference information such as lists of irregular verb forms, non-action (stative) verbs, pronouns, and a chart of modal meanings. Students should be reminded to refer to this information in related lessons.

Photo Credits

Unit 1
Page 1: © Viorika Prikhodko/iStockPhoto
Page 8: © Aldo Murillo/iStockPhoto
Page 15: © Friday/Dreamstime.com
Page 28: © Rene Mansi/iStockPhoto
Page 35: © altrendo images/Getty Images
Page 38: Top left: © Mikael Andersson/Photolibrary; Top right: © Phil Boorman/Getty Images; Left center: © David Lewis/iStockPhoto; Right Center: © Photos.com/RF; Bottom left: © Kmitu/Dreamstime.com
Page 42: © altrendo images/Getty Images
Page 47: © PhotosToGO

Unit 2
Page 53: © Hill Street Studios/Blend Images/Getty Images
Page 57: © Hill Street Studios/Blend Images/Getty Images
Page 61: © Photos.com/RF
Page 66: © Dallaseventsinc/Dreamstime.com
Page 69: Left: © Photos.com/RF; Right: © Rafael Botto/iStockPhoto
Page 70: © Sue Wilson/Alamy
Page 72: © Amir Niknam Pirzadeh/iStockPhoto
Page 73: Top left: © John247/Dreamstime.com; Top left center: © Zasada/Dreamstime.com; Top right center: © Paula Connelly/iStockPhoto; Top right: © Achim Prill/iStockPhoto; Bottom left: © Doug Schneider/iStockPhoto; Bottom left center: © Shawn Gearhart/iStockPhoto; Bottom right center: © Kae Horng Mau/iStockPhoto; Bottom right: © Operative401/Dreamstime.com
Page 74: Top left: © Emelie Lindback/iStockPhoto; Top left center: © Aleksandr Lobanov/iStockPhoto; Top right center: © Nruboc/Dreamstime.com; Top right: © Sang Nguyen/iStockPhoto; Bottom left: © xyno/iStockPhoto; Bottom center: © Palto/iStockPhoto; Bottom right: © Mshake/Dreamstime.com
Page 76: © John.59/Dreamstime.com
Page 80: © Urosr/Dreamstime.com
Page 91: © Iakov Filimonov/iStockPhoto
Page 95: Left: © Iakov Filimonov/iStockPhoto; Center: © Foto.fritz/Dreamstime.com; Right: © Kentannenbaum/Dreamstime.com
Page 97: © Photos.com/RF
Page 103: © Hofmeester/Dreamstime.com
Page 108: © Joeygil/Dreamstime.com
Page 111: © Photos.com/RF

Unit 3
Page 112: © Photos.com/RF
Page 115: © Lemonpink/Dreamstime.com
Page 119: Top: © David M. Albrecht/Shutterstock; Center: © Photos.com/RF; Center: © Dutchy/iStockPhoto; Bottom: © Otokimus/Dreamstime.com
Page 120: © Juanmonino/iStockPhoto
Page 126: © Dorothea Lange/Corbis
Page 133: © Coral Coolahan/iStockPhoto
Page 140: © Monkeybusinessimages/Dreamstime.com

Unit 4
Page 148: © Corbis Premium RF/Alamy
Page 152: © Stuart McClymont/Getty Images
Page 156: © Photos.com/RF
Page 160: © Chris Schmidt/iStockPhoto
Page 161: Top: © Jon Feingersh/jupiterimages; Center: © Gehringj/Dreamstime.com; Center: © Niderlander/Dreamstime.com; Bottom: © Dmitriy Shironosov/iStockPhoto
Page 164: © Photos.com/RF
Page 171: © Deanna Bean/iStockPhoto
Page 176: Left: © Jeffrey Smith/iStockPhoto; Right: © Nyul/Dreamstime.com
Page 182: © PhotosToGO
Page 186: © Ana Abejon/iStockPhoto
Page 190: Top: © Jacob Wackerhausen/iStockPhoto; Bottom: © Sebcz/Dreamstime.com

Unit 5
Page 191: © PhotosToGO
Page 198: © Ant236/Dreamstime.com
Page 207: © Joselito Briones/iStockPhoto
Page 214: © manley620/iStockPhoto
Page 217: © Chris Schmidt/iStockPhoto
Page 221: © Tangducminh/iStockPhoto
Page 225: © Sswartz/Dreamstime

Unit 6
Page 230: © Anyka/iStockPhoto
Page 236: © Anyka/Alamy
Page 237: © Vasic/Dreamstime.com
Page 243: © Chaoss/Dreamstime.com
Page 252: © 1920 (color litho) Crane, Walter (1845–1915), (after) / Private Collection/ Ken Walsh/The Bridgeman Art Library
Page 265: © Barbara Sauder/iStockPhoto

Contents

APPENDICES 273

INDEX 285

Imperatives/Commands

Important Information for Students
1. Follow the rules and expectations for each class.
2. Read the syllabus carefully for homework assignments.
3. Do not miss classes or assignments.

Presentation

Questions

1. Circle the verb in sentences 1 and 2 on the list of *Important Information for Students.* Write the two words you circled.

   _____

   _____

2. Do you see the endings *-s* or *-ed* on these verbs? What is the subject of these verbs?

3. Circle the verb in sentence 3. Why is the word *do* in this sentence?

Explanation—Imperatives/Commands

1. Every sentence in English must have a subject (**who** or **what** you are talking about) and information about that subject. Also, a complete sentence needs a subject and a verb.*

2. The sentences on the list in the presentation above do not have subjects. These verbs are *commands* or *imperatives,* and the subject is an **understood** *you.* In other words, the reader or listener understands or knows the subject is *you,* so we do not need to include it in the sentence.

3. An imperative (or command) uses the simple or base form of the verb only. We do not add any endings (such as *-s* or *-ed*) to the verb.

   Follow the rules and expectations for each class.
   Read the syllabus carefully for homework.

_____

*(Review sentence patterns in *Destinations 1 Writing for Academic Success*—Unit 1, pp. 8–10.)

4. To make a negative imperative or command, add the auxiliary (helping verb) **do** and the word **not** before the verb.

   Do not miss classes or assignments.

   Do not come to class unprepared.

Follow this pattern for negative sentences with commands/imperatives:

auxiliary (helping verb)	*not*	verb (simple/base form)	
Do	not	miss	classes or assignments.
Do	not	come	to class unprepared.

5. In conversation, native speakers often use contractions with *do* and *not*.

   Don't miss classes or assignments.

   Don't come to class unprepared.

   NOTE: You should use contractions in conversation only. We do not usually use them in formal writing.

6. We use the imperative form of the verb in several situations as follows:

   - to give instructions   *Read* the syllabus carefully for homework.
   - to give advice   *Study* the chapter for the test tomorrow.
   - to make requests   *Send* me an email to remind me.
   - to give directions   *Walk* straight ahead to get to the library.

7. Sometimes we use commands in more serious situations or as warnings. The speaker often wants to be very direct in these cases.

   Sit quietly in your chair!   *Don't talk* to other students during a test!

You may need to be careful when you want to use commands, depending on the situation. In some situations you may want to be more polite and not so direct. In these cases other words (such as "please") will help you be more polite.

   Please sit quietly in your chair now.

PRACTICE

Activity 1

Circle the imperative verb form in each sentence. In one sentence you should circle two imperative verbs. If a sentence is negative, circle the words that work with the verb to make it negative.

 EXAMPLE: (Come) to class on time.

1. Know and understand each instructor's course rules.

2. See your instructor during his/her office hours.

3. Do not have many absences in any class.

4. Listen to all the instructor's announcements in class.

5. Do not leave class early.

6. Bring assignments to class by the due date.

 Activity 2

Fill in the imperative form of one of the verbs from the list. In some cases, make the sentences negative as indicated. Use each verb only one time.

 VERBS: ask   forget   send   go   use   be   call

When you are absent from class . . .

1. _____ a friend in the class for notes and homework.

2. _____ the instructor an email.

3. _____ about new assignments.

4. _____ to get missed assignments. *(negative)*

5. _____ responsible for completing any missed work.

6. _____ to the instructor during his/her office hours.

7. _____ your absence as an excuse to miss work. *(negative)*

Activity 3

In textbooks there are many kinds of exercises and activities with different instructions. Match each Instruction (1–8) with an Example (a–h). Follow the example.

	INSTRUCTIONS		EXAMPLES
_f_	1. Mark each statement *T* or *F.*	a.	<u>Respect</u> other people's opinions.
___	2. Put a check next to the command.	b.	*Give* other people a chance to speak.
___	3. Circle the imperative verb form.	c.	~~You~~ listen to other people's opinions.
___	4. Put two lines under the imperative verb.	d.	✓Don't talk at the same time as others.
___	5. Fill in the space with a command form of the verb.	e.	Raise <u>your hand to answer a question</u> .
___	6. Correct the mistake with the imperative.	f.	_F_ Always shout out an answer in class.
___	7. Choose the imperative form.	g.	(Participate/~~Participated~~) in class regularly.
___	8. Complete the instruction.	h.	(Ask) your teacher for help.

 Activity 4

A. *Each of the following sentences has a mistake with a verb form. Find the mistakes and correct each one. The first one has been done as an example.*

What to do if you arrive late to class:

1. Please find~~s~~ a seat quickly.

2. Announce not the reason that you are late.

3. You sit near the door if possible.

4. No walk across the front of the class.

5. Sit quietly and tries to catch up with the lesson.

6. You not disturb others by asking questions.

B. *This is a phone conversation between a student and his instructor. Find four mistakes with imperatives and show how to correct them.*

Student: Hello. This is Jason Edwards, and I'm in your English 100 class. I'll miss class today because of an appointment with my doctor.

Instructor: You'll need today's assignment to prepare for the next class. Sees me during my office hour between 3 p.m. and 4 p.m. to get that paper.

Student: I have a class at that time. Can I get it another time?

Instructor: I can leave it in an envelope on my door. You pick it up any time after 3 p.m., but not try to get it before then. Also, don't you hand in this assignment late. It's important to do this before the quiz next week.

 Activity 5

A. *Write an instruction or piece of advice for a new student using the information given in parentheses on each Line "a" below. Use the imperative form of the verb in each sentence.*

B. *Then write a negative instruction or piece of advice for a new student using the information given in parentheses on each Line "b" below. Use the imperative form of the verb in each sentence.*

You may also need to add some of your own words in these sentences. Follow the example.

1. a. (take advantage of / instructor's office hours) Take advantage of your instructor's office hours.

    b. (be shy) Don't be shy.

2. a. (come / class / regularly) _____

    b. (be / absent) _____

3. a. (catch up on / missed work) _____

    b. (forget about / assignments) _____

4. a. (arrive / each class / on time) _____

    b. (arrive / late) _____

5. a. (pay attention to / teacher's announcements) _____

   _____

   b. (have private conversations / classmates)_____

   _____

6. a. (turn off / cell phone) _____

   b. (answer / calls / your cell phone)_____

7. a. (stay / in class / entire time) _____

   b. (leave / class / early)_____

Activity 6

A. *Look at the map of a college campus. Give directions to and from the following places next to each number below. Use the imperative form of the verbs from the box in your directions. Follow the example.*

VERBS: turn   make   walk   follow   continue   take   go

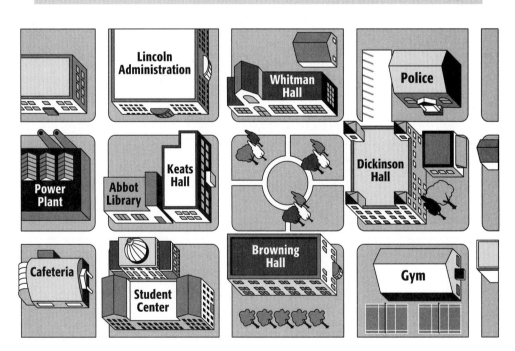

EXAMPLE: From Keats Hall to the cafeteria

Walk out of Keats Hall and turn right. Go to the corner and make

another right. Walk straight to the next corner. Take a left and

you will see the cafeteria on the right side of the street.

1. From Keats Hall to the library

_____

_____

2. From the cafeteria to the Lincoln Administration

_____

_____

3. From the gym to the student center

_____

_____

4. From the power plant to the police station

_____

_____

B. *Ask another student to give you directions to and from the same places. Compare your answers.*

Past Time

Simple Past

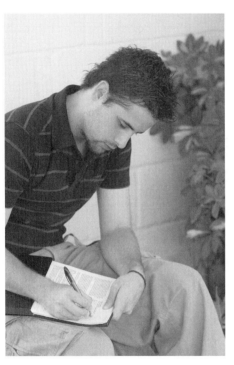

[1]Alberto **started** his college education last semester. [2]First, he **completed** the application process, and then he **took** assessment tests in English and math. [3]He **received** the results of those tests on his registration day. [4]He **did not register** for his classes without those results.

Presentation

Questions

1. Look at the verbs in bold in sentences 1, 2, and 3. What ending do you see on most of these words?

   Circle the verb in bold that does not have this ending. Why is this verb different?

2. What is the time in this paragraph? How do you know? What specific words tell you the time?

3. Look at the words in bold in sentence 4. What is the verb in this sentence? Why is the word *did* in this sentence?

Explanation—Past Time: Simple Past

1. **Regular verbs: verb + -*ed*.** We call these verb forms *simple past.*

   Alberto *started* his college education last semester.
   He *registered* for his classes.

2. **Spelling changes with the -*ed* ending.**

The chart below shows spelling rules for simple past verb forms.

Simple (base) form of verb	Spelling rule	Examples	
Most regular verbs	Add the -*ed* ending.	register	register**ed**
		start	start**ed**
Ends in the letter -*e*	Add -*d* only.	use	use**d**
		announce	announce**d**
Ends in a consonant + -*y*	Change the -*y* to -*ie*	study	stud**ied**
		hurry	hurr**ied**
Ends in a vowel + -*y*	Add the -*ed* ending.	stay	stay**ed**
		enjoy	enjoy**ed**
Is one syllable and ends in consonant/vowel/consonant	Double the final consonant and add -*ed*	stop cvc	stop**ped**
		plan cvc	plan**ned**
a) Has two syllables b) Ends in consonant/vowel/consonant c) Last syllable is stressed (stronger)	Double the final consonant	prefer' cvc	prefer**red**
		control' cvc	control**led**
a) Has two syllables b) Ends in consonant/vowel/consonant c) Last syllable is not stressed	Add the -*ed* ending. (Do not double a letter.)	en'ter cvc	enter**ed**
		lis'ten cvc	listen**ed**
Ends in -*w*, -*x*, or -*y*	Add the -*ed* ending. (Do not double a letter.)	show	show**ed**
		fix	fix**ed**
		stay	stay**ed**

3. Some verbs do not use the -*ed* ending for past time. These verbs are called *irregular* verbs. You must memorize these irregular forms. (See the Appendix list of irregular verbs, page 273.)

> He *took* assessment tests in English and math. He *got* the test results quickly.

4. Other words in a sentence can also tell you past time. Some of these time words are:

> *yesterday*   *last week/month/year*
>
> *ago* (*three days ago/long ago*)   *a specific year* (2006)

5. **Negative sentences**

To make a negative sentence with these simple verbs, add the auxiliary (helping verb) *did* and the word *not* before the verb. Use the simple/base form of the verb. Do <u>not</u> add the *-ed* ending to the verb (or use the irregular past form) in this case.

He *did not (didn't*) choose* his classes without his test results.

He *did not (didn't*) register* without his test results.

Follow this pattern for negative sentences with past tense verbs:

subject	auxiliary (helping verb)	*not*	verb (simple form)	
He	did	not	choose	his classes carefully.
He	did	not	register	without his test results.

NOTE: Do not use *did* when a form of *be* is the main verb. See Unit Two in both *Destinations 1 Writing and Grammar* books for more information about *be* as a main verb.

Practice

Activity 1

Read the two paragraphs in A and B below. Find and write all the simple past verb forms in the chart below. Write each verb in the correct column of the chart. Find and write the negative verbs in the column on the right.

A. Ana <u>registered</u> for four classes at her local community college last week. She used her school's registration system on the Internet. She thought that the process was easy. However, she <u>did not succeed</u> in getting all of her first-choice classes. Two of the classes did not have any open seats, so she put her name on a wait list for those classes.

B. Last summer Glenn met with his counselor to talk about his future classes. They discussed Glenn's goals and objectives. Then the counselor suggested some basic courses in math and English. Glenn agreed because he did not want to take anything too challenging for his first semester in college. He chose a beginning algebra class and a reading class. He did not choose any other classes for the new semester.

Regular	Irregular	Spelling change	Negative
registered			did not succeed

---

*Native speakers of English often use contractions in conversation. We do not usually use contractions in formal writing.

Activity 2—Verbs with Spelling Changes   (Review sentence patterns in *Destinations 1*
Writing for Academic Success—Unit 1, pp. 8–10.)

A. *Fill in the blank spaces with the past form of the verbs in parentheses. Be
    sure to make spelling changes when necessary.*

Gladys last (attend) _____ school five years ago, so her
₁

math class last semester (challenge) _____ her. She
₂

(worry) _____ about tests in that class. She (receive)
₃

_____ some help from tutors at the Math Lab. Then she
₄

(pass) _____ all her tests.
₅

B. *Circle the correct verb in parentheses. Remember to think about spelling
    changes.*

1. My friend (skipped / skiped) too many English classes. His instructor
    (droped / droppd / dropped) him from the class.

2. George (listened / listenned) to his counselor's advice about classes to
    take last year. He (pland / planned / planed) his schedule carefully with
    her help.

3. Selena's friends (wanted / wantted / wantd) her to take a music class
    with them. She (preferred / prefered) to take a photography class.

4. Bob (askked / asked) his instructor for permission to hand in his paper a
    day late. The instructor (permittd / permited / permitted) him to do this.

Activity 3—Irregular Verbs

A. *Fill in the spaces in the paragraph with the past form of the irregular verbs in parentheses. One answer will be negative.*

Paula (have) _____ an excellent schedule this past
    1

semester. She (spend) _____ a long time planning her
    2

classes around her children's school schedules. She (take)

_____ advantage of their hours in school and (find)
    3

_____ classes in the mornings only. During her breaks
    4

between classes, she (read) _____ her assignments. She
    5

also (write) _____ her papers in the writing lab. This (give)
    6

_____ her a chance to complete much of her work at
    7

school. When she (come) _____ home, she (have –
    8

negative) _____ too much school work to do.
    9

B. *Complete the two paragraphs on this and the next page with the past tense of the verbs in the list. One verb will be negative. The verbs may fit in more than one space, but use each verb only one time.*

VERBS:	know	choose	spend	begin	get	drive

1. Last week José _____began_____ his first semester of college. He
    1

_____ two classes on Mondays and Wednesdays in
    2

the morning and one evening class on Tuesdays. He *(negative)*

_____ the campus well, so he _____ to
    3   4

school early on Monday. He _____ there an hour before
    5

class. Then he _____ over half an hour looking for
    6

parking.

VERBS:	feel	meet	give	draw	forget

2. On the first day of school, José _____ his campus map.
   ₁
   Fortunately, some people _____ him directions to his
   ₂
   classrooms. One person _____ a small map to show the
   ₃
   walk from one classroom to the other. He also _____
   ₄
   another student in the same two classes on Monday and Wednesday
   mornings. At the end of the day, José _____ good about
   ₅
   his first day of classes at this new school.

Activity 4

*Each of the following sentences has one mistake with a simple past verb form.
Find the mistakes and show how to correct them. Your correction may involve
more than one word. Follow the example in the first sentence.*

       completed
1. Yesterday John ~~completeed~~ his history homework during his English
   class. He pay not attention to the English lesson. The instructor become
   upset with him.

2. Cindy arrivved late to her 9 a.m. class this morning. She did not heard
   the teacher's announcement about the quiz tomorrow.

3. Joe camed to his biology class last night without preparing the
   homework.

4. Janet goed to her instructor's office after class last week. She not
   understood the chapter.

5. John's advisor refered him to a higher level math class. John studied
   every day for that class.

Activity 5 (Review sentence patterns in *Destinations 1 Writing for Academic Success*—
Unit 1, pp. 8–10.)

A. Write sentences about this class or your work in this class using simple past verbs. Use any of the subjects and verbs in the following lists. Be sure to use a different subject and verb in each sentence. Use the past time word or expression in parentheses.

B. After you write your sentences, make each one negative. Write these sentences on the line below the time word or expression. Follow the examples.

| Subjects: | the instructor | the students | I | we |
| | my classmates | another student | | |

| Verbs: | study | review | explain | assign | bring |
| | teach | complete | try | plan | |

EXAMPLES:

A. (early this morning)   I woke up early this morning to study.

B.   I didn't wake up early this morning to study.

1. a. (last week) _____

   b. _____

2. a. (yesterday) _____

   b. _____

3. a. (the first day of class) _____

   b. _____

4. a. (a few days ago) _____

   b. _____

5. a. (last night) _____

   b. _____

Past Time

Questions with Simple Past

¹Did this student **register** on time for this semester? **²Did** her friends **take** classes too? **³When did** they **register** for classes?

Presentation

Questions

1. Why is the word *did* in sentences 1 and 2? How is the word order in these questions different from a statement?

2. How is the third question different from the first two?

3. What kind of information will be in the answer to the first two questions? What kind of information will be in the answer to the last question?

Explanation—Questions in Past Time

1. *Yes/No* questions—The answer will be *yes* or *no*.

    To make a question with simple past verbs:

    a. Add the auxiliary (helping verb) *did* before the subject (to the left of the subject).
    b. Use the simple/base form of the verb. Do <u>not</u> add the *-ed* ending to the verb (or use the irregular past form) in this case.
    c. End the sentence with a question mark.

    Did this student *register* on time for this semester?
           subject   verb

    Did her friends *take* classes too?
         subject verb

Follow this pattern for *yes/no* questions with past tense verbs:

auxiliary (helping verb)	subject	verb (simple form)	end with question mark
Did	this student	register	on time for this semester?
Did	her friends	take	classes too?

2. **Question word questions**—The answer will be a piece of information.

   To make a question with simple past verbs:

   a. Add the question word and *did* before the subject (to the left of the subject).
   b. Use the simple/base form of the verb. Do <u>not</u> add the *-ed* ending to the verb (or use the irregular past form) in this case.
   c. End the sentence with a question mark.

   When did they *register* for classes?   *Why did* they *take* a math class?
   subject   verb   subject verb

Follow this pattern for question word questions with past tense verbs:

question word	auxiliary (helping verb)	subject	verb (simple form)	end with a question mark
What	did	you	find	online about the class?
When	did	they	register	for classes?
Why	did	they	take	a math class?
Where	did	the class	take	the field trip?
How	did	you	complete	the assignment?
			verb (simple past)	
Who*			took	a math class?
What*			challenged	your friend?

*NOTE: Do not use *did* when the question word replaces the subject.
Also, do not use *did* when a form of *be* is the main verb in the sentence.
(Refer to Unit 2 in *Destinations 1 Writing for Academic Success* for more information about *be* as a main verb.)

Practice

Activity 1   (Review sentence patterns in *Destinations 1 Writing for Academic Success*—
Unit 1, pp. 8–10.)

*Match the questions on the left with the answers on the right. Put a check (✓)
at the end of the* yes/no *questions. Put an* X *at the end of the information
questions.*

_____ 1. Did you take Professor Smith's
Art 101 class last semester?

_____ 2. When did you go to the lab
to type your paper?

_____ 3. Who helped you with that
difficult assignment last week?

_____ 4. Did all the students complete
the project on time?

_____ 5. Why did some students fail
the assignment?

a. They didn't follow
the professor's instructions
carefully.

b. My friend shared his notes
from that class with me.

c. No, some students brought
it after the due date.

d. No, I took that course from
a different professor.

e. Yesterday after class I had
some extra time.

Activity 2

A. *Complete the following* yes/no *questions using one of the verbs from the list
below in simple past. Use a different verb for each sentence. Follow the
example.*

| VERBS: | discuss | forget | close | print | take | tell |

1. _____Did_____ you _____forget_____ your pen at home this morning?
You can borrow mine.

2. _____ your classmates _____ their goals in the Personal
Development 98 class?

3. _____ the instructor _____ the disruptive students to
be quiet?

4. _____ you _____ all the pages of the report to hand
in today?

5. _____ the online computer system _____ a long time
for your registration?

6. _____ the testing office _____ early today?

B. *Complete the following question word questions using one of the verbs from the list below in simple past. Use a different verb for each sentence.*

VERBS:	type	expect	say	assign	read	tell

1. Where _____ you _____ the guidelines for this class?

2. When _____ the instructor _____ that big report?

3. How _____ the students _____ their homework so quickly on the computer?

4. Who _____ you about tomorrow's test?

5. What _____ the instructor _____ about tomorrow's test?

6. Why _____ some students _____ this class to be difficult?

Activity 3

Correct one mistake in each question below. Be sure to make each one a question and not a statement. Follow the example.

EXAMPLE: Did your speech communication instructor discussed her syllabus during the first class?

1. When she did explain the objectives for the course?

2. What the students thought about the first class?

3. Your classmates did feel free to ask questions?

4. Who did ask questions about the group project?

5. Why some students had trouble understanding the teacher?

6. Most of the students brought the textbook to the first class?

Activity 4 (Review sentence patterns in *Destinations 1 Writing for Academic Success*—
Unit 1, pp. 8–10.)

Change the order of the words above each line to make a good question. Add punctuation and capitalization. Do not add any other words to your sentences. Follow the example.

1. your history class / you / go / did / yesterday / to

   Did you go to your history class yesterday?

2. the instructor / did / say / to you / what

   _____

3. to you / give / she / did / the new assignment

   _____

4. explain / the instructor / the rules / of her class / did / again

   _____

5. come / did / why / you / without the work / to class

   _____

6. gave / those tips / about the math homework / who / to you

   _____

7. did / grade / your late assignment / how / the instructor

   _____

8. did / your math instructor / include on the test / last week / what

   _____

Activity 5

One student is asking another student questions about a class he took. On each blank line below write a question that fits the underlined information in the answer. Use a past tense verb in each question. Follow the example.

EXAMPLE:

Student 1:   *Where did you study French ?*

Student 2:   I took a beginning class in it <u>at this school</u>.

1.   Student 1:   _____

   Student 2:   I took it <u>last year during the fall semester</u>.

2.   Student 1:   _____

   Student 2:   I took it <u>because I needed to fulfill a language requirement</u>.

3.   Student 1:   _____

   Student 2:   It was <u>Dr. Jehlen</u>, but I think she retired last semester.

4.   Student 1:   _____

   Student 2:   We mostly <u>practiced conversation</u>.

5.   Student 1:   _____

   Student 2:   <u>I listened to a CD of French conversations</u> every day for a week.

6.   Student 1:   _____

   Student 2:   <u>No</u>, I got a B in that class, but I was happy with that.

General/Habitual Time

Simple Present

City College
Spring Semester 2009
ESL 100 - Section 5502
Tuesday/Thursday 9:30 am -11:45 am Room 257
Tuesday 1:30 pm – 2:20 pm ESL Lab 70-122

Instructor: Cynthia Parks

Office: 575B

Phone: 555-0567

E-Mail: Cynthia.Parks@ccnc.edu

OFFICE HOURS:

MONDAY	TUESDAY	WEDNESDAY	THURSDAY	FRIDAY
3:00 – 4:00 pm	12:30 – 1:30 pm	10:30-11:30 am 3:00 – 4:00 pm	12:30 – 1:30 pm	By appointment

Required Text
Herzfeld-Pipkin   *Destinations 1-Writing*   Heinle 2007
Herzfeld-Pipkin   *Destinations 1- Grammar*   Heinle 2009

Other Course Materials
• folder/notebook for handouts   • blue book – **large size** (for journal writing)

You should also have an **English-English** dictionary..

Course Description
This is the second course in the study of English grammar, reading and writing for ESL students. The students will study and practice grammar, write sentences, and paragraphs, and practice reading skills. In addition, they will spend one hour a week in the ESL Lab in order to reinforce and develop grammar, reading, and writing skills introduced in class.

Student Learning Outcomes
Upon successful completion of this course, students will have the skills to:

• compose organized and developed intermediate-level paragraphs on a variety of personal and academic topics

• correctly apply grammatical structures as listed in the core level scope and sequence chart for ESL 100.

[1]Instructors **establish** specific rules for their classes. [2]Each instructor usually **provides** a syllabus with these rules during the first week of class. [3]A syllabus always **gives** important information and guidelines for a class. [4]Sometimes new students **do not realize** the importance of the information in the syllabus.

Presentation

Questions

1. On the lines below write the subject of each bold verb in sentences 1, 2, and 3.

_____ establish

_____ provides

_____ gives

   Do all of these verbs have the same ending? If not, how are they different?

2. Look at sentences 2, 3, and 4 for any time words. Circle these words. What is the time of these sentences?

3. Look at sentence 4. Why is the word *do* in this sentence?

Explanation—Simple Present

1. **Simple form of verb or verb + -s.** We call this *simple present*.

   Add the *-s* ending only when the subject is he/she/it or a single item (third person singular).

   Instructors establish specific rules for their classes.

   A syllabus always *gives* important information.

2. **Spelling changes with the *-s* ending.**

The chart below shows spelling rules for the simple present *-s* ending. Remember these endings are only for she/he/it or a single item as subjects.

Simple (base) form of verb	Spelling rule	Examples	
Most verbs	Add the *-s* ending	provide	provide**s**
		give	give**s**
		want	want**s**
Ends in a consonant + *-y*	Change the *-y* to *-ie*	study	stud**ies**
		hurry	hurr**ies**
Ends in a vowel + *-y*	Add the *-s* ending.	stay	stay**s**
		enjoy	enjoy**s**
Ends in *-s, -x, -z, -sh,* or *-ch*	Add *-es*	establish	establish**es**
		fix	fix**es**
		pass	pass**es**
Ends in *-o*	Add *-es*	do	do**es**
		go	go**es**

3. The name for these verb forms is *simple present,* but we do not usually use them for present time (now or right now). We use these verb forms for things people do regularly or as a routine, such as habits and customs. We also use them to talk about scientific facts. The time in these sentences is **general** or **habitual** time.

    An instructor usually *provides* a syllabus during the first week of class.

    Water boils at 212° F (100° C) and freezes at 32° F (0° C).

4. We can use several time words or expressions to show general or habitual time.

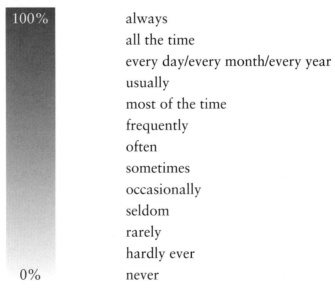

100%	always
	all the time
	every day/every month/every year
	usually
	most of the time
	frequently
	often
	sometimes
	occasionally
	seldom
	rarely
	hardly ever
0%	never

We often place these words between the subject and verb of the sentence. Sometimes you will find them at the beginning or end of a sentence.

A syllabus *always* gives important information and guidelines for a class.

Sometimes new students do not realize the importance of the information in the syllabus.

5. **Negative sentences**

To make a sentence negative using a simple present verb form, add the auxiliary (helping verb) *do* or *does* and the word *not* before the verb. Do <u>not</u> add the *-s* ending to the verb in this case.

Sometimes new students *do not (don't*) realize* the importance of the information in the syllabus.

Sometimes a new student *does not (doesn't*) realize* the importance of the information in the syllabus.

Follow this pattern for negative sentences in general or habitual time (using a simple present verb):

subject	auxiliary (helping verb)	not	verb (simple form)	
New students	do	not	realize	the importance of a syllabus.
A new student	does	not	realize	the importance of a syllabus.

NOTE: Do not use *do* or *does* when a form of *be* is the main verb. See Unit 2 in both *Destinations 1 Writing and Grammar for Academic Success* for more information about *be* as a main verb.

Practice

Activity 1   (Review sentence patterns in *Destinations 1 Writing for Academic Success*— Unit 1, pp. 8–10.)

Circle the subject and verb of each sentence below. If the verb is negative, include all words that go with the negative verb, such as do, does, *and* not *in your answer. Put a line under time words or expressions in these sentences. The first one has been done as an example.*

1. <u>Sometimes</u> (students choose) only one or two classes to enroll in. Often they do not have time for too many classes because of work or family.

2. Other students enroll in twelve units or more each semester. A student with financial aid usually establishes a full schedule. She/He does not want to break the rules for getting this money.

---

*Native speakers of English often use contractions in conversation. We do not usually use contractions in formal writing.

3. An international student always carries a full load of classes because of
    visa requirements. Each student becomes full time with his/her study
    visa. These students do not usually qualify for financial aid. However,
    they sometimes receive scholarship money.

Activity 2

A. *Fill in the blank spaces with the correct form of the verb. Be sure to make
    spelling changes when necessary. Some answers will be negative. Circle any
    general/habitual time words or expressions in these paragraphs. Follow
    the example.*

1. Rogerio (usually) (try) _____tries_____ to take afternoon
                                      a
    classes. Sometimes he (sleep) _____ late and
                                              b
    (miss) _____ a class. His roommates (take)
                      c
    _____ classes earlier in the day. They (see–*negative*)
              d
    _____ him before school.
            e

2. Amara often (worry) _____ about tests and quizzes. She
                                  a
    (study) _____ as much as possible when an instructor
                    b
    (announce) _____ one. She always (pass)
                        c
    _____ her exams. Her children (understand–*negative*)
            d
    _____ her worrying.
            e

B. *Complete the two paragraphs below with the present tense form of any of
    the verbs in the list above the paragraph. Some verbs will be in the negative
    form. Use each verb only one time. Follow the example.*

VERBS:	think	make	relax	miss	call	finish

1. Berta _____makes_____ a study routine at the beginning of each
                    a
    semester. She _____ her homework assignments before
                            b
    dinner. Then she _____ for the evening, and she
                              c
    (*negative*) _____ about school. Sometimes Berta's friends
                          d
    _____ her for information when they _____
            e   f
    a class.

VERBS: give   send   wait   want   reply   answer

2. Most of the time that instructor _____ to email very
    _a

    quickly. For example, students _____ their questions to
    _b

    her in the morning, and she _____ before the afternoon
    _c

    classes. She (negative) _____ until the next day to
    _d

    answer their questions, even on the weekends. She also frequently

    _____ her students tips about preparing for tests. She
    _e

    _____ to help each student succeed.
    _f

Activity 3

Find and correct eleven mistakes with present tense verbs in a student's journal entry below.

I often observes the other students in my classes, and
sometimes their actions surprises me. First of all, most
students payes attention to the teacher at all times, but a
few students doesn't always listen. Sometimes these
students talk to the people around them, and these
conversations becomes disruptive to the whole class. Also, a
few students come to class without the homework. Then
they not participate in our discussions about the answers.
One student come late to class almost every day. Then he
doesn't understands the work, so he askes many questions.
Another student occasionally leave early or don't return to
class from the break.

Activity 4   (Review sentence patterns in *Destinations 1 Writing for Academic Success*—
Unit 1, pp. 8–10.)

A. *On the lines below write sentences about how often you do the activities given. Use a time word/expression from the list below in each of your sentences. You may also add some of your own words to these sentences. Follow the example.*

always	frequently	usually	often
sometimes	rarely	hardly ever	never

EXAMPLE: I usually type all my homework assignments on the computer.
type homework assignments on the computer

1. _____
study with a classmate or group of students

2. _____
review the textbook before a test

3. _____
miss more than one or two classes in a semester

4. _____
relax after school

5. _____
look at my notes after class

6. _____
complete assignments before the due date

B. *Turn to the person next to you and share your answers. Ask your classmate to tell you about his or her activities. Write your classmate's answers on the lines.*

EXAMPLE: Jin rarely studies with a classmate._____

1. _____
2. _____
3. _____
4. _____
5. _____
6. _____

Activity 5

Write five sentences about yourself or your classes on the lines below using simple present tense. Make one sentence negative. Use a different word from each of the three lists below in each of your sentences. Add your own words as well. Follow the examples.

List A—Verbs:

follow	understand	pay attention to	take advantage of
read	hand in	give	assign

List B—Nouns:

guidelines	objectives	goals	syllabus
expectations	on time	tips	homework

List C—Time Words:

always	often	usually	sometimes
rarely	seldom	never	

EXAMPLES: I always read each class syllabus several times.

My math instructor usually doesn't assign homework the night

before a test.

1. _____

_____

2. _____

_____

3. _____

_____

4. _____

_____

5. _____

_____

General/Habitual Time

Questions with Simple Present

¹**Do** these students **enjoy** their discussion groups? ²**Does** each student **have** a chance to participate in every class? ³**Why does** the instructor **ask** them to work in small groups?

Presentation

Questions

1. Why is the word *do* used in sentence 1? Why is the word *does* used in sentence 2? What kind of questions are they: *yes/no* or question word questions?

2. How is the third question different from the first two? What kind of question is it?

Explanation—Questions with Present Tense Verb Forms

1. *Yes/No* questions—The answer will be *yes* or *no*.

   To make a question with simple present verbs:

   a. Add the auxiliary (helping verb) *do* or *does* before the subject (to the left of the subject). Use *does* only for she/he/it or other single item (third person singular).
   b. Use the simple/base form of the verb. Do <u>not</u> add the *-s* ending to the verb in this case.
   c. End the sentence with a question mark.

      Do the students *enjoy* their discussion groups?
             subject   verb

      Does each student *have* a chance to participate in every class?
              subject   verb

Follow this pattern for *yes/no* questions with present tense verbs:

auxiliary (helping verb)	subject	verb (simple form)	end with question mark
Do	the students	enjoy	their discussion groups?
Does	each student	have	a chance to participate in every class?

2. **Question word questions**—The answer will be a piece of information.

   To make a question with simple present verbs:

   a. Add the question word and *do* or *does* before the subject (to the left of the subject).
   b. Use the simple/base form of the verb. Do <u>not</u> add the *-s* ending to the verb in this case.
   c. End the sentence with a question mark.

   Why does the instructor *ask* them to work in small groups?
   subject   verb

Follow this pattern for question word questions with past tense verbs:

question word	auxiliary (helping verb)	subject	verb (simple form)	end with a question mark
Why	does	the instructor	ask	them to work . . . ?
When	do	the students	speak	in that class?
What	does	that student	say	about the class?
Where	does	the class	meet	on Tuesdays?
How	do	the students	form	discussion groups?
			verb (simple present)	
Who*			assigns**	the groups?
What*			helps**	the students?

*NOTE: Do not use *do* or *does* when the question word replaces the subject.
    Also, do not use *do* or *does* when a form of *be* is the main verb in the sentence.
    See Unit 2 in both *Destinations 1 Writing and Grammar for Academic Success* for more information about
    be as a main verb.
**Always use the verb + *-s* form in these questions.

Practice

Activity 1 (Review sentence patterns in *Destinations 1 Writing for Academic Success*—Unit 1, pp. 8–10.)

Match the answers to the questions below according to the information on the chart.

Admissions and Records	Monday through Thursday 8:00 AM to 7:00 PM Friday 8:00 AM to 3:00 PM
Counseling Center	Monday through Thursday 8:00 AM to 7:00 PM Friday 8:00 AM to 3:00 PM
Testing/Assessment	Monday through Thursday 8:00 AM to 7:00 PM Friday 8:00 AM to 12:00 PM

_____ 1. Does the testing office have the same hours as the other two offices?

_____ 2. When do the counselors finish work on Fridays?

_____ 3. Who leaves at noon on Fridays?

_____ 4. Do the counselors work on the weekends?

_____ 5. What office gives tests on the weekends?

_____ 6. What time do these offices open?

a. The assessment office gives tests only on weekdays and never on weekends.

b. They all open at 8:00 a.m. Mondays through Fridays.

c. No, they only work Monday through Friday.

d. They go home at 3:00 p.m.

e. The testing office workers leave at that time.

f. No, it closes earlier on Fridays.

Activity 2

A. *Circle the correct choice for each space to make a* yes/no *question. Follow the example.*

EXAMPLE: ((Do) / Does) those students always (enjoys / (enjoy)) their group discussions?

1. (Do / Does) Phillip usually (participates / participate) in his group?

2. (Do / Does) all instructors (require / requires) class participation as part of the class grade?

3. (Do / Does) each student frequently (succeed / succeeds) in participating in the class?

4. (Do / Does) everyone in the class (understand / understands) the instructor's expectations about class participation?

5. (Do / Does) most students (feels / feel) free to ask questions in the class?

B. *Complete the following question word questions using one of the verbs from the list below in simple present. Use a different verb for each sentence. Follow the example.*

VERBS: assign   register   find   contact   meet   teach   go

EXAMPLE: When _____*does*_____ the class _____*go*_____ to the writing lab?

1. Where _____ the class _____ on lab days?

2. Who _____ that class?

3. What kind of homework _____ the instructor always

    _____ students to complete?

4. How _____ students _____ the instructor with questions?

5. Why _____ students often _____ that class challenging?

6. When _____ students _____ for that lab class?

Activity 3

A new student is asking questions about a local college. Find and correct one mistake in each question. Follow the example.

EXAMPLE: How ~~does~~ students register for classes?

1. Does the Admissions Office accepts online applications?

2. When the new schedule of classes does come out each semester?

3. Does new students need to take many tests?

4. What does students need to take to the Admissions Office?

5. When new students attend an orientation?

6. Who does help students with their plan for classes?

 Activity 4   (Review sentence patterns in *Destinations 1 Writing for Academic Success*— Unit 1, pp. 8–10.)

 Rearrange the words to form a good question. No new words need to be added to the sentences. There might be more than one correct answer. Include punctuation and capitalization. Follow the example.

EXAMPLE: Do you always find a buddy in each of your classes?
find / you / always / a buddy / in each of your classes / do

1. _____
your buddy / does / in your history class / you / help / how

2. _____
students / in their classes / form / often / do / study groups

3. _____
meet / usually / does / your new study group / where

4. _____
does / assign / sometimes / group projects / your biology instructor

5. _____
the number of groups / decides / who / for the class

6. _____
does / divide / how / the students / into groups / the instructor

Activity 5

A. *Read the following parts of a syllabus and ask questions about this information.*

1. Write a *yes/no* question on Line a about the information given.
2. Write an information question on Line b about the information given.

Use as many different information words as possible in your answers on Line b.

EXAMPLES:

a. Does the instructor collect assignments at the end of class?

b. What do students need to complete on time?

I.   Homework/Assignments:

*   Students need to complete all homework/assignments on time.
*   The instructor always collects assignments at the beginning of the class period only.
*   In general, the instructor does not accept late homework.

a. _____

b. _____

II. Journals:

*   Students in this class write in their journals every week.
*   The instructor collects these and responds to them.
*   Students receive credit for completing the assignments on time.

a. _____

b. _____

III. Written Assignments:

*   Assignment due dates are important! Pay attention to these dates!
*   The instructor allows students to turn in **one** late paper during the semester without penalty. Students lose points for other late work.
*   Students lose one grade for each class their work is late.
*   The instructor accepts typed papers only.

a. _____

b. _____

B. *Exchange your questions with a partner. Answer your partner's questions with full sentences below. Your partner will answer your questions in the same way.*

1. _____

    _____

2. _____

    _____

3. _____

    _____

4. _____

    _____

5. _____

    _____

6. _____

    _____

Present Time

Present Progressive (Continuous*)

Presentation

[1]Right now the instructor **is starting** a new lesson in this class, and some students **are listening** carefully. [2]Other students **are taking** notes. [3]One student **is reading** a text message on her cell phone. [4]She **is not trying** to pay attention to the instructor now.

Questions

1. Look at the words in bold in sentences 1, 2, and 3 above. What do you see at the end of each verb? Which words in bold are working with the main verbs in these sentences?

2. Below are the words in bold from sentences 1, 2, and 3. Write the subject of each of these in the spaces next to the words.

    _____ is starting   _____ are taking

    _____ are listening   _____ is reading

3. Look at the bold words in sentence 4. How are they different from the words in bold in all the other sentences?

4. What is the time of this paragraph? How do you know this? (What words tell you about the time?)

Explanation—Present Progressive (Continuous*)

1. Present progressive = present of the auxiliary (helping verb) *be (am/is/are)* + verb + *-ing*

    Be sure to have all three of these parts (*be* + verb + *-ing*).
                    1   2   3

    a. The form of *be* must agree with the subject of the sentence.

---

*NOTE: Some books use the word *continuous* and not *progressive*. Progressive and continuous have the same meaning.

    b. The verb must have the *-ing* ending. The *-ing* ending on the verb tells you the action is continuous or not finished.

        The **instructor** *is starting* a new lesson in this class.
               1   2   3

        Some **students** *are listening* carefully.
              1   2   3

2. Spelling changes with the *-ing* ending.

    The chart below shows spelling rules for present progressive verbs.

Simple (base) form of verb	Spelling rule	Examples	
Most verbs	Add the *-ing* ending.	start	starting
		listen	listening
Ends in the letter *-e*	Drop the *-e*. Add *-ing*.	use	using
		announce	announcing
Is one syllable and ends in consonant/vowel/consonant	Double the final consonant and add *-ing*	stop CVC	stopping
		plan CVC	planning
a) has two syllables b) ends in consonant/vowel/consonant c) last syllable is stressed (stronger)	Double the final consonant	admit CVC	admitting
		control CVC	controlling
a) has two syllables b) ends in consonant/vowel/consonant c) last syllable is not stressed	Add the *-ing* ending. (Do not double a letter.)	enter	entering
		listen	listening
Ends in *-ie*	Change the *-ie* to *-y*. Then add the *-ing*.	tie	tying
		lie	lying
		die	dying

3. Use these verb forms for present time or actions that are taking place now/at the moment.

    Time words that usually indicate present time:

    now   right now   at the moment   at present   today

EXAMPLES:

Right now the instructor *is starting* a new lesson in this class.

All the students *are trying* to pay attention *today*.

4. We also use present progressive to talk about something that is in progress or not finished over a longer period of time. We call this *extended present*.

    Time words that can indicate extended present:

    this week   this semester   this month   this year

    EXAMPLES:

    This semester we *are studying* paragraph writing.

    This week that student *is practicing* verb forms at the computer lab.

5. **Contractions**—Speakers often use contractions in conversation with these verbs.

    | I am | I'm listening | s/he is | s/he's listening |
    | you are | you're listening | we are | we're listening |
    | they are | they're listening | | |

    REMINDER: We do not usually use contractions in formal writing.

6. **Negative sentences**

    Add the word *not* after the auxiliary (helping verb) *be* to make a sentence negative.

    The instructor *is not (isn't*) starting* a new lesson.

    Some students *are not (aren't*) taking* notes.

    Follow this pattern for negative sentences with present progressive verbs:

subject	auxiliary (helping verb) (be)	not	verb + *-ing*	
The instructor	is	not	starting	a new lesson.
Some students	are	not	taking	notes.

---

*Native speakers often use contractions in conversation. We do not usually use these forms in formal writing.

Practice

Activity 1   (Review sentence patterns in *Destinations 1 Writing for Academic Success*—Unit 1, pp. 8–10.)

Put the letter of the sentence next to the matching picture below. Then make each sentence negative. Write the negative sentences on the lines under the pictures.

   a. The instructor is filing her papers in the file cabinet very carefully.
   b. A student is opening the door.
   c. A problem is occurring on the computer.
   d. They are waiting for class to begin.
   e. Students are running to get to class on time.

1. _____

2. _____

_____

3. _____

4. _____

_____

5. _____

_____

Activity 2

Fill in the spaces with the present progressive form of the verb in parentheses. You will need to make some of your answers negative.

Right now some students (attend) _____ a new student

orientation at their school. They (prepare) _____ to register
₂

for classes for next semester.

- A counselor (give) _____ information about the online
₃

  registration process. He (stop–*negative*) _____ for
₄

  questions.

- Several students (read) _____ some guidelines about
₅

  registering on the computer. They (listen–*negative*) _____
₆

  to the counselor.

- One student (make) _____ a chart of his new schedule.
₇

  He (refer) _____ to the printed schedule of classes for
₈

  information.

- Another student (locate) _____ her classrooms on a
₉

  campus map. She (put) _____ an *X* on all of the buildings
₁₀

  of her classes.

Activity 3

Find five mistakes with present progressive verbs in each paragraph. Show how to correct each one.

A. Right now José is sit at a computer in the writing lab at school. He is

   completeing an assignment for his Speech 120 class. He is saves all of

   his changes, but he no is printing any of his work right now. He is

   planing to check everything for mistakes first.

B. Julianna is no writing any of her assignments for school by hand this

   semester. Instead, she are taking advantage of her school's writing lab,

   and she is typeing everything on computers there. Her friends are using

   not computers for most of their assignments. They is spending too

   much time to write and revise all of their work.

Activity 4   (Review sentence patterns in *Destinations 1 Writing for Academic Success—*
Unit 1, pp. 8–10.)

*A class is ending right now. Write sentences about what is happening in this
classroom using the words under each line. Be sure to use present progressive
verbs and include correct capitalization and punctuation. Follow the example.*

1. Two students are leaving the room as quickly as possible.
   leave / two students / as quickly as possible / the room

2. _____
   from the board / start / the instructor / the homework assignments / to erase

3. _____
   the homework assignment / one student / in his notebook / write

4. _____
   the instructor's notes / copy / from the board / some students

5. _____
   enter / students / the room / to wait for the next class

6. _____
   into his backpack / put/ another student / all his papers and books

Activity 5   (Review sentence patterns in *Destinations 1 Writing for Academic Success—*
Unit 1, pp. 8–10.)

*The students in the following pictures are doing things differently today than they
usually do. Each picture shows their usual activities next to today's activities.*

A. *Write a sentence using the words under each picture to describe what they
   usually do using simple present verbs.*

B. *Write another sentence about what they are doing today using present
   progressive verbs.*

C. *Write a third sentence about what they are not doing using negative present
   progressive. Follow the example.*

EXAMPLE:

A. Usually Juliana takes the bus to school.

B. Today she is riding her bicycle to school.

C. *(negative)* Today Juliana is not taking the bus to school.

1.

    A. Usually these students _____

    B. This semester they _____

    C. *(negative)* This semester these students _____

2.

    A. Usually Ahmad _____

    B. Today he _____

    C. *(negative)* Today Ahmad _____

3.

    A. Usually Bob and Alice _____

    B. This semester they _____

    C. *(negative)* This semester Bob and Alice _____

4.

    A. Usually Rosa _____

    B. Today she _____

    C. *(negative)* Today Rosa _____

Present Time

Questions with Present Progressive

¹**What is** this instructor **doing** in class today? ²**Is** she **starting** a new lesson? ³**Are** all the students **taking** notes?

Presentation

Questions

1. Look back at the sentences about the picture in Lesson 6 (page 35). Look at the sentences under the photo here. How is the word order different in these sentences from the sentences in Lesson 6?

2. Circle the *yes/no* questions under the photo and put a line under any question words in a question.

3. What is the time in these questions? How do you know this?

Explanation—Questions with Present Progressive (Continuous) Verbs

1. *Yes/No* **questions**—The answer will be *yes* or *no*.

    To make a question with present progressive verbs:

    a. move the auxiliary (helping verb) *be (am/is/are)* to the left of the subject.
    b. keep the *-ing* on the verb.
    c. end the sentence with a question mark.

    Is the instructor *starting* a new lesson today?
       subject   verb

    Are some students *taking* notes?
       subject   verb

    Follow this pattern for *yes/no* questions with present progressive verbs:

auxiliary (helping verb)	subject	verb + *-ing*	end with question mark
Is	the instructor	starting	a new lesson today?
Are	some students	taking	notes?

2. **Question word questions**—The answer will be a piece of information.

   To make a question with present progressive verbs:

   a. begin the sentence with the question word.
   b. move the auxiliary (helping verb) *be (am/is/are)* to the left of the subject.
   c. keep the *-ing* on the verb.
   d. end the sentence with a question mark.

   Why is the instructor *starting* a new lesson today?

   Where are the students *practicing* the verb forms?

   Follow this pattern for question word questions with present progressive verbs:

question word	auxiliary (helping verb)	subject	verb (simple form)	end with a question mark
Why	is	the instructor	starting	a new lesson today?
Where	are	the students	practicing	the verb forms?
How	are	some students	taking	notes?
What	is	that student	telling	his friend?
			verb (present progressive)	
Who*			is teaching	the students?

   *NOTE: Do not change the word order when the answer is the subject. *Also, always use the singular form "is" with these questions.*

Activity 1   (Review sentence patterns in *Destinations 1 Writing for Academic Success*—Unit 1, pp. 8–10.)

Match the questions on the left with the answers on the right.

_____ 1. Is that instructor teaching Music 101 this semester?

_____ 2. When is the instructor giving the midterm this semester?

_____ 3. Who is visiting the class today?

_____ 4. Where is the class meeting today?

_____ 5. Why are some students working at the computers in the library today?

_____ 6. Are the students in Joe's class taking a tour of the library today?

a. He is not sure. He said probably during the eighth week of classes.

b. The instructor is taking the class to the computer lab.

c. No, he is teaching Music 150 and 200.

d. Yes. They are not meeting at the regular classroom today.

e. A special speaker is coming to talk.

f. They are preparing a big assignment for their economics class.

Activity 2

A.   *Complete the following* yes/no *questions using one of the verbs from the list below in present progressive. Use a different verb for each sentence. Some verbs may fit more than one sentence. Follow the example.*

VERBS:	look	ask	put	take	research	wait

EXAMPLE: _____ *Is* _____ that class _____ *taking* _____ a tour of the library today?

1. _____ some students _____ in line to see the librarian?

2. _____ one student _____ the librarian for some help?

3. _____ Janet and Hector _____ the Internet for information?

4. _____ the instructor _____ some books on reserve this semester?

5. _____ those students _____ for a book on reserve?

B.   *Complete the following question word questions using one of the verbs from the list below in present progressive. Use a different verb for each question.*

VERBS:	say	find	get	go	talk

1. Where _____ the students _____ for class today?

2. Why _____ they _____ a tour of the library?

3. How _____ they _____ information for their papers?

4. Who _____ _____ too loudly in the library right now?

5. What _____ the librarian _____ to the disruptive students?

Activity 3

Find and correct ten mistakes with present progressive verbs in the following conversation between two students.

Kyle: Hi Suzanne. What are you do right now? Is you studying for the vocabulary midterm?

Suzanne: Yes. I am refering to the review sheet from the instructor. You reviewing all of the chapters on that paper?

Kyle: Yes, I am reads all of them again. How you are memorizing all of the idioms?

Suzanne: I am making flash cards, one card for each idiom.

Kyle: We do studying so many of them this semester. Is the flash cards helping?

Suzanne: Yes, I learning all of them fairly easily this way.

Activity 4   (Review sentence patterns in *Destinations 1 Writing for Academic Success*— Unit 1, pp. 8–10.)

Change each of the following sentences into yes/no *questions. Follow the example.*

> **EXAMPLE:** Some students are taking a chemistry test right now.
>
> *Are some students taking a chemistry test right now?*

1. They are trying to follow all of the instructor's tips about test taking.

   _____

2. Several students are reading the instructions carefully.

   _____

3. Alicia is using her time wisely.

   _____

4. She is looking ahead at all the pages to see the total number of questions.

   _____

5. She is also only spending a few minutes on each question.

   _____

Activity 5

Write questions using present progressive verbs and question words. The answers to your questions are underlined in each statement. Follow the example.

1. One student is skipping <u>the difficult questions</u>.

   What is one student skipping? _____

2. Some students are working <u>very slowly</u>.

   _____

3. All the students are taking the test <u>in the chemistry lab</u>.

   _____

4. One student is answering only the easier questions <u>to save time</u>.

   _____

5. <u>Robert</u> is going back to the more difficult questions now.

   _____

Non-Action (Stative) Verbs

¹Right now Barbara **is preparing** for next week's classes. ²She **wants** to read the new chapter in the textbook now because she **has** some free time. ³She **does not know** her work schedule for next week. ⁴Therefore, she **is trying** to take care of her schoolwork today.

Presentation

Questions

1. What is the time of this paragraph? How do you know this? What words tell you this?

2. Look at the verbs in bold in sentences 1 and 4. What verb forms are they?

3. Look at the verbs in bold in sentence 2. Why are they a different verb form from the verbs in sentences 1 and 4?

4. Why is the word *does* with the verb in bold in sentence 3?

Explanation—Non-Action (Stative) Verbs

1. In Lesson 6 you learned about present progressive (continuous) verb forms. We use these forms for actions taking place now or in present time.

   Some verbs do not use the *-ing* ending. They cannot be in the progressive (continuous) form because they are not actions. These verbs are called *non-action* or *stative* verbs.

   > She *wants* to read the new chapter in the textbook now. She *has* some free time today.

2. The following groups show some common stative verbs.

emotions:	*hate like love dislike trust*
mental states:	*know remember forget believe/feel* *think understand mean*
state of being:	*be feel*
perceptions and senses:	*hear see smell taste seem sound look*

needs and preferences: *want need prefer hope*

measurements: *cost weigh contain*

possession: *own possess belong have*

3. Sometimes you will see the progressive *-ing* ending on some of these verbs. The use of this ending depends on the meaning.

   a. **think**

      1. When the meaning is *believe* and it expresses an opinion, do not use the progressive.

         The students *think* the syllabus has a lot of information.

         The instructor *thinks* the students understand the syllabus.

      2. When you have ideas in your head and you are thinking **about** something, you can use the *-ing* ending.

         I *am thinking* about my schedule for next semester.

         He *is thinking* about the advice from his counselor.

   b. **have**

      1. When you want to show ownership, do not use the progressive.

         You *have* a lot of books for that class. My friend *has* some lab supplies to give me.

      2. When you use specific expressions such as *have a party, have a good time, have a problem, have a test,* you can use the *-ing* ending.

         We *are having* a test in this class today. My friend *is having* a problem in his lab class.

   c. Some other verbs on the list above also sometimes use the *-ing* ending. Some examples are:

      taste: This food *tastes* delicious. I *am tasting* the food to see if it needs salt.

      feel: I *feel* nervous, but she *feels* calm about the test. I *am feeling* the keyboard for dirt or grease.

      weigh: My books *weigh* several pounds. I *am weighing* these vegetables to figure out the price.

      smell: The chemicals in the lab *smell* terrible. I *am smelling* this chemical before I use it.

      look: You *look* happy today. She *is looking* for her lost lab notes.

Practice

Activity 1   (Review sentence patterns in *Destinations 1 Writing for Academic Success—*
Unit 1, pp. 8–10.)

A. *Circle all the non-action (stative) verbs in the paragraph below. If
a non-action verb is negative, circle the words that go with the verb
to make it negative as well.*

B. *Put a line under the verbs using the -ing progressive ending. Follow
the examples.*

Richard <u>is using</u> the computers in the lab this semester because he

(doesn't own) a computer right now. He has one in his house, but it belongs

to his sister. She wants to get it back soon. Richard understands this

problem. However, he doesn't have enough money to buy one right now.

He is thinking about this situation, and he is trying to find a solution.

Activity 2

Circle the word in each parentheses that fits the sentence.

Rolf (is / are) (has / having) trouble finding a good place to study today.
    1   2

He (am / is) (try / trying / tries) to find a good spot in his house.
      3   4

He (is needing / needs) a quiet place with no disruptions. He (are / is)
              5   6

(going / goes / go) from room to room to look for a quiet corner. The
      7

kitchen (is seeming / seems / seem) quiet, but he (smells / is smelling) all
                  8   9

the good food there. He (is thinking / thinks) that he cannot study there
                                    10

right now. The living room (doesn't / isn't) (has / have) anyone in it,
                                      11   12

but he (is hearing / hears) the loud music from the room next door.
              13

He (is thinking / think / thinks) about going to school now because he
                14

(know / is knowing / knows) a quiet place to study there.
              15

W *Activity 3* (Review sentence patterns in *Destinations 1 Writing for Academic Success*— Unit 1, pp. 8–10.)

A. *Fill in each blank space with either a simple present or present progressive form of the verb in parentheses. Some answers will be negative.*

Irma (register) _____ for classes right now, but she (have)
1
_____ a problem. She (want) _____ a
2   3
Monday/Wednesday art class. However, it (have–*negative*)

_____ any seats left. She (know) _____ she
4   5
can register for a night class. She (prefer) _____ to go
6
to school during the day only. She (like–*negative*) _____ to
7
come home late at night by herself. Her friends (tell) _____
8
her to put her name on a wait list. She (think) _____ that
9
she can find the teacher to ask about adding that class.

B. *Fill the spaces in the paragraph with the simple present or present progressive form of a verb from the list below. Some answers will be negative. Use each verb only one time.*

VERBS: want trust follow remember prepare need continue

Marcy and Andy _____ a project for their history class
1
today. They _____ the instructions, but they (*negative*)
2
_____ all the details of the assignment. Andy
3
_____ to go home soon, so he _____ to
4   5
work on it. Marcy (*negative*) _____ her memory. She
6
_____ to call a classmate to find out the rest of the
7
information.

Activity 4

Find twelve mistakes in the following paragraph and show how to fix them.

Right now Carmela is shop at the bookstore for her books and school

supplies. She looking at the prices of everything. It all seem very expensive.

Each book is costing at least $40, and she is needing two books for most of

her classes. Now she is understanding why people talk about the expense of books for college. In addition, some books feels very heavy. She is thinking that they are weighing too much for her small backpack. She realize that she is needs something else to carry her books, but she isn't have anything with her.

Activity 5 (Review sentence patterns in *Destinations 1 Writing for Academic Success*—Unit 1, pp. 8–10.)

Write five sentences about what is happening or what you see in the following picture using the verbs in the list below it. At least one of the five sentences should be negative. Use a different verb from the list in each sentence.

VERBS:	like	understand	hear	smell	seem	
	sound	look	prefer	cost	contain	have

1. _____

    _____

2. _____

    _____

3. _____

    _____

4. _____

    _____

5. _____

    _____

Nouns

Singular/Plural/Proper Nouns

[1]These two **students** are wearing several **kinds** of **decorations** on their **bodies**. [2]He is wearing **earrings**. [3]She has a permanent **tattoo** on her **arm** and a pierced **lip**.

Presentation 1

Questions

1. Look at all the bold words in these sentences. Circle the singular words (*singular* = one of something).

2. Which of the bold words in these sentences are plural (*plural* = more than one of something)? How do you know this?

Explanation—Singular and Plural Nouns

1. A noun can be a person, place, thing, or idea. A noun can be *singular* (one item) or *plural* (more than one item). We use an *-s* ending to make a noun plural.

   1 kind—2 kinds

   one design—three designs

   one culture—many cultures

2.   Spelling changes with the -s ending.

The chart below shows spelling rules for the plural noun -s ending.

Noun	Spelling rule	Examples	
Most nouns	Add the -s ending	kind	kinds
		culture	cultures
		design	designs
Ends in a consonant + -y	Change the -y to -ie	body	bod**ies**
		society	socie**ties**
		story	stor**ies**
Ends in a vowel + -y	Add the -s ending	day	days
		boy	boys
Ends in -s, -x, -z, -sh, or -ch	Add -es	class	classes
		tax	taxes
		watch	watches
Ends in -o	Add -es for some nouns	hero	heroes
		tomato	tomatoes
		potato	potatoes
	Other nouns add only -s	zoo	zoos
		radio	radios
		piano	pianos
Ends in -f(e)	Some nouns drop -f and add -ves	life	lives
		knife	knives
		wife	wives
	Exceptions:	belief	beliefs
		chief	chiefs
		roof	roofs

3.   Some common nouns in English are irregular. This means they do not use the -s ending in the plural form.

man/men   woman/women   child/children   tooth/teeth

person/people   mouse/mice   foot/feet

Other nouns do not change form. In other words, they have the same form for both singular and plural.

deer   fish   sheep   shrimp

Chinese   Japanese   Vietnamese   Swiss

4. Some nouns are always in pairs in English as follows:

    glasses   pajamas   scissors   trousers/pants/jeans/slacks/shorts

5. Sometimes you will find certain words before a singular or plural noun as follows:

    Singular   *one* (*one* tattoo)   *a* or *an* (*a* tattoo/*an* earring)

    (See Lesson 17, pages 112–113 for more information about the articles *a* and *an*.)

    Plural   a number more than one (*two* tattoos/*ten* tattoos)

    several (*several* tattoos)   *some* (*some* tattoos)   *many* (*many* tattoos)

    (See Lesson 11, page 66 for more information about these words.)

6. A noun can be in several places in a sentence.

    a. It can be a subject or an object. It also can follow a preposition.

        The *man* has an *earring* <u>in</u> his *ear*.
           subject   object   object of preposition

        Those *students* have *tattoos* <u>on</u> their *arms*.
           subject   object   object of preposition

        Remember to make the verb in the sentence agree in number with the subject.

        That ***man*** *is* a chief.   Those ***men*** *are* chiefs.
          noun/subject   nouns/subjects

    b. A noun can also follow a linking verb and show identification.
        (See *Destinations 1 Writing for Academic Success*, Unit 2, pages 39–44 for a review.)

        The man with a tattoo <u>is</u> *a chief*.
                    linking verb

        Both the man and woman <u>are</u> *students*.
                    linking verb

Practice

Activity 1

Put a line under each singular noun and circle each plural noun. Follow the examples.

Many (people) from different cultures decorate their bodies. Each <u>group</u> may have a different style or tradition for this. One society may make temporary marks, but another group may make permanent changes, such as tattoos or pierced ears and lips. In some places a person may choose an individual way to look attractive.

Activity 2

Write the plural form of each word in parentheses on the line given after it.
Follow the examples.

   EXAMPLE: They put (line) ____lines____ on their (cheek) ____cheeks____ .

1. He uses (ash) _____ to make black (dot) _____ on
    his face.

2. Some (lady) _____ wear no makeup at all.

3. Some (person) _____ wear interesting
    (hairstyle) _____ .

4. She likes to wear (feather) _____ in her hair.

5. Some (chief) _____ are (hero) _____ .

6. Some (warrior) _____ may carry (knife) _____ .

7. You can use the (leaf) _____ of those (plant) _____ to
    make some (basket) _____ .

8. Some (picture) _____ tell stories.

9. (Woman) _____ put henna on their (hand) _____ and
    (foot) _____ .

10. He takes (class) _____ in anthropology to learn about different
    (society) _____ .

Activity 3   (Review sentence patterns in *Destinations 1 Writing for Academic Success—*
            Unit 1, pp. 8–10 and Unit 2, pp. 39–45.)

*A. Circle the subject and the correct verb in parentheses to agree with that
    subject in each sentence below. Follow the examples.*

Each (culture) ((has) / have) different meanings for body art. Today this

practice (is / are) a mixture of old traditions and new practices. Often
              1

people (travel / travels) or (moves / move) to many parts of the world. We
        2   3

also (has / have) better communication between different areas these days.
     4

Therefore, materials, practices, and designs (moves / move) through
                                               5

different cultures. A traditional kind of art (gets / get) new meaning as it
                                               6

(goes / go) across cultural and social *boundaries.* Therefore, changes in   limit/edge
 7

decoration (is / are) common.
            8

B. *Circle the subject of each sentence. Then fill in the spaces with the correct form of the verb to fit that subject. Follow the example.*

Many (people) (like) _____*like*_____ to wear tattoos. Both men and
                                 1

women (put) _____ permanent pictures or designs on their
                        2

skin. This (be) _____ a very old tradition. Sometimes scientists
                       3

(find) _____ tattoos on mummies in different parts of the
                4

world. For example, a European mummy named Otzi (have)

_____ tattoos on several parts of his body, and a Peruvian
           5

female mummy still (wear) _____ tattoos on her arm.
                                     6

Presentation 2

Joe Russo and **Marla Abungin** live in **Canada**. They are
students at **Canyon College**, and they are studying digital arts.
They met last **September** in their **Photography** 150 class.

Explanations—Proper Nouns

Some nouns always begin with a capital (large) letter.
These nouns are called *proper nouns*.

The chart on this page and page 58 shows types of proper nouns. These names
require capital letters.

Names of people and their titles	John Lane Mr. John Lane
	Emma Snowden Ms. Emma Snowden
	Felicia Martinez Dr. Felicia Martinez
Note: Do not capitalize the title without the name of the person.	I spoke to **Professor Singh**.
	I spoke to my professor.
Names of places:	
• cities	They live in **Vancouver**.
• states/provinces	She lives in **California**.
• countries	They found a mummy in **Peru**.
• continents	Someone found a mummy in **Europe**.
• oceans	The **Pacific O**cean is very deep.
• lakes	**Lake Erie** is one of the **Great Lakes**.
• rivers	The **Hudson River** runs into the **Atlantic Ocean**.
• deserts	The **Gobi Desert** is in **Asia**.
• mountains	The **Alps** are in several countries in **Europe**.

Names of • streets • buildings • parks/zoos/museums	It's on the corner of **M**ain **S**treet and **F**ifth **A**venue. **S**torm **H**all is near the **L**earning **R**esource **C**enter. I love to visit the **S**an **D**iego **Z**oo.
Names of • businesses • schools • courses (but not names of subjects)	**C**oca **C**ola and **P**epsi are in many countries. I am taking classes at **G**rossmont **C**ollege. She loves her **A**nthropology 200 class. She takes an anthropology class every semester.
Names of • months • days • holidays	This class started in **J**anuary. We always have a quiz on **M**ondays. We don't work on **I**ndependence **D**ay.
Names of • languages • nationalities • religions	She speaks both **E**nglish and **C**hinese. They follow **K**orean customs. There are many religions in the world, such as **I**slam, **B**uddhism, **C**hristianity, **J**udaism, and **H**induism. **M**uslims pray several times a day.

Activity 4

Match the nouns on the left with the places or people on the right. Use each letter only one time. Then circle all the proper nouns. Follow the example.

___d___ 1. henna designs

_____ 2. makeup

_____ 3. Irezumi tattoos

_____ 4. Ta Moko tattoos

_____ 5. the word "tatau"

_____ 6. lip and ear lobe disks

_____ 7. Tahiti

a. Japanese

b. island in the Pacific

c. word from Polynesia

d. (Hindu) bride

e. African tribeswoman

f. Maori warrior from New Zealand

g. North American women

Activity 5

Read the following journal entry of a student and capitalize the first letter of all the proper nouns. Then circle all the other nouns in the paragraph. Follow the examples.

I love A̧ (anthropology) 102 because my instructor, dr. soto,

makes every class very interesting. Today we learned about a

mummy named otzi the iceman. In september, 1991 two

germans found a body over five thousand years old in the ice

on a mountain. Scientists named this man otzi because

these tourists from germany found him in the otzal alps

between italy and austria. Scientists studied this man

carefully for many years. During these studies they found

about 57 tattoos on the lower back and left ankle as well as

behind the right knee. The body now sits on display at the

south tyrol museum of archaeology in the city of bolzano,

italy. I love to study anthropology, and I plan to take another

class in it next semester.

Activity 6

A. *Find the following kinds of mistakes and show how to correct each one.*

- 4 proper noun capitalization mistakes
- 7 mistakes with singular or plural nouns

The moche persons lived many year ago in ancient peru. Several year ago some scientist found a very old mummy (1600 years old) of a moche Woman. They found symbols of power on her, such as a crowns with a supernatural face and many tattoo on one arms.

B. *Find the following kinds of mistakes and show how to correct each one.*

- 2 verb mistakes   • 7 mistakes with singular or plural nouns

The mummy's tattoos was pictures of several snake and spider. These creatures often symbolize different kind of agricultural rituals. They also found something called *cinnabar* on her bodies. This are a red minerals. In addition, they found some earring and a necklaces near her.

Activity 7   (Review sentence patterns in *Destinations 1 Writing for Academic Success*—
Unit 1, pp. 8–10 and Unit 2, pp. 39–45.)

A. *Answer the following questions about the information in Activities 5 and 6.
Write complete sentences and underline all the nouns in your answers. Then
write one question of your own for each paragraph.*

Information about Otzi the Iceman (from Activity 5)

1. What name did scientists give the mummy in the Alps?

    _____

2. What did scientists find on the body of this mummy?

    _____

3. Where is the body of this mummy now?

    _____

4. Your question: _____

    _____

Information about the Moche Mummy (from Activity 6)

1. Who were the Moche people?

    _____

2. How old is the mummy of the Moche woman?

    _____

3. What did they find on her arms?

    _____

4. Your question: _____

    _____

B. *Compare your answers with a partner. Ask your partner to write an answer
to each of your questions in this activity.*

Nouns

Count/Non-Count

Presentation

Questions

1. Circle all the nouns in these sentences with the plural *-s* ending.

2. Look at all the nouns in bold. Why do you think these words do not have the *-s* ending?

[1]This woman likes to look nice for **work**. [2]On weekday mornings she puts some **makeup** on her eyes and **jewelry** on her ears and neck. [3]She also puts a little **oil** on her **skin** to try to look young.

Explanation—Count/Non-Count Nouns

1. Some nouns are *countable* or *count* nouns. This means you can count them or think of them as individual or separate items. These nouns follow the rules for plurals you discussed and practiced in Lesson 9.

   1 eye—2 eyes   one morning—five mornings   one woman—many women

2. Some nouns are *uncountable* or *non-count* nouns. We don't think of these things as separate or individual. This is because these items are often too small to count, or they are activities or conditions.

   The following list shows some uncountable nouns in English.

Liquids:	coffee, tea, water, milk, oil, paint, perfume, gasoline
Small, granular things:	sugar, sand, rice, salt, pepper, other spices (like cinnamon), earth, dust
Materials:	gold, cotton, wood, glass, steel, plastic, rubber, coal, soap, clay
Gases:	air, pollution, smog, oxygen

Some food items:	bread, fish, cheese, meat, chicken, beef, lamb, butter, yogurt, soup, cereal
Ideas/feelings: (Abstract nouns)	knowledge, intelligence, health, truth, honesty, courage, wealth, peace, happiness, trouble, luck, fun, life, beauty, love, hate, time
School subjects:	mathematics, physics, economics, biology, psychology, history, chemistry, engineering, French, Spanish, English, Chinese
Other:	advice, grammar, vocabulary, communication, information, news, work, homework, traffic, transportation, weather, rain, snow, crime, help, hair, work, agriculture, garbage, noise, education, experience, music, art

3. Non-count nouns will not have a plural form. Do not add an -s ending to these nouns. The verb in the sentence with these nouns will be singular.

    The *makeup* on her eyes *is* colorful.

    The *oil* from that vegetable *is* good for your skin.

4. Some non-count nouns are types or groups of things. The type or group is uncountable, but the individual parts in the group are usually countable.

Type/ Group	Individual Parts
Jewelry:	necklaces, rings, bracelets, pins
Clothing:	shirts, blouses, sweaters, coats, ties, skirts, dresses
Furniture:	chairs, tables, lamps, desks
Money:	coins, bills, dollars, quarters, nickels, dimes
Homework:	exercises, assignments, essays, paragraphs, sentences
Fruit:	apples, oranges, pears, grapes, berries
Some other groups are:	equipment, food, makeup, mail

Practice

Activity 1

Circle the non-count nouns and put a line under the countable nouns.

1. There are many ways to show beauty.

2. Often people use their knowledge of natural materials to decorate their bodies.

3. Men and women in different societies wear specific kinds of jewelry and clothing for rituals and celebrations.

4. They sometimes wear these things for luck.

5. Other times they use these items to show wealth.

Activity 2 (See *Destinations 1 Writing for Academic Success,* Unit 2, pages 39–44 for a review of subject-verb agreement with count and non-count nouns.)

Circle the correct word in each set of parentheses in the following sentences.

1. Sometimes body (arts / art) (show / shows) a culture's artistic expression.

2. A warrior's (courage / courages) (seems / seem) strong with face and body decorations.

3. (Golds / Gold) (are / is) a typical material to insert into nose piercings in some cultures.

4. The Moche woman's (hair / hairs) (was / were) in a traditional style of braids.

5. Sometimes (advice / advices) about special makeup (is / are) important.

Activity 3 (Review sentence patterns in *Destinations 1 Writing for Academic Success*— Unit 1, pp. 8–10 and Unit 2, pp. 39–45.)

Below is a list of different things people use for decorating their bodies. Fill in the space for the subject of each sentence with one of these items. Use each item only one time. Then write the correct form of the verb in parentheses to fit the sentence. Follow the example.

charcoal	powder	ink	juice	jewelry	wood	clay	paint

EXAMPLE: _____Jewelry_____ often (go) _goes_ into a pierced lip or ear lobe.

1. _____ (color) _____ the skin to make a tattoo.

2. In some cultures _____ (become) _____ a disk to insert in a pierced ear or nose.

3. White or yellow _____ often (make) _____ skin color lighter.

4. _____ from a specific kind of fruit (be) _____ a kind of makeup in some parts of the world.

5. In some places _____ (come) _____ from the leaves of certain plants.

6. _____ (leave) _____ black marks on the skin.

7. _____ (be) _____ still a kind of body paint in some areas of the world.

Activity 4

Find 12 mistakes (9 with nouns and 3 with verbs) in the following conversation. Show how to correct each one.

Angela: Hi, Tim. I had some troubles with my car today, so I was absent from our economics class. Did I miss any important informations?

Tim: It was a good classes. We spent a lot of times reviewing several chapter in the textbook. The instructor also assigned some homeworks.

Angela: Uh oh. Do I have a lot to catch up on?

Tim: The works are a little bit difficult, and there are a lot of vocabularies to study.

Angela: I may need some helps from you if that's okay.

Tim: Economics are a difficult subject. I can give you all my note from class, but maybe you should contact the instructor also.

Angela: That's a good ideas. I'll call you back after I talk to her. Thanks.

Activity 5

A. *Think about some rituals or celebrations in your culture. Then look at the list of non-count nouns below. Do you use any of these things in those rituals or celebrations?*

    Add any other non-count nouns you may use to this list.

    Non-count nouns:

rice	tea	coffee	water	oil	paint	perfume
money	gold	clothing	glass	bread	health	noise
advice	music	hair	wood	makeup	jewelry	

    Other non-count nouns: _____

B.   *Write some count nouns of things you use in the same rituals in your culture from section A on the line provided. Follow the examples in the box.*

Count nouns:

guest	bride	groom	ring

_____

C.   *Write three sentences discussing the use of these items. You can write about one ritual or celebration or more than one, but each sentence should include different nouns from both lists A and B. Follow the examples.*

EXAMPLES: Sometimes guests throw rice at a wedding,

A bride and groom often give rings at a wedding.

1. _____

_____

2. _____

_____

3. _____

_____

Quantity

Quantifiers/Units of Measurement

[1]There are **many lines** in these designs. [2]There is only **a little space** for more lines because there is **a great deal of henna** *paste* on these hands. [3]This woman is also wearing **several bracelets**. [4]She **doesn't have any rings** on her fingers.

mixture of powder and water

Presentation 1—Quantifiers

Questions

1. Circle the nouns in bold in sentences 1, 2, and 3. Label each one count or non-count.

2. What words come before the count nouns and what words come before the non-count nouns? Write these words below in the correct box.

Words before *count* nouns
Words before *non-count* nouns

3. What word in bold is a noun in sentence 4? What word comes before this noun? How is this sentence different from the other three sentences?

Explanation—Words/Expressions of Quantity— Quantifiers

1. We use several words or expressions with nouns to tell us how much or *quantity*. Some of these words and expressions are *indefinite quantifiers*. We use these with non-count nouns because they will not have a specific number. We can also use indefinite quantifiers with count nouns when we do not want to use a specific number.

2. Some indefinite quantifiers may be the same for count and non-count nouns, and others may be different.

    Below is a chart of some common indefinite quantifiers to use with nouns.

Count Only	Non-Count Only	Both Count and Non-Count
a couple of	a little	no
a few	a great deal of	any
several	much	some
many		a lot of
		lots of/plenty of (informal)

3. We usually use *much* in negative sentences and questions only. We often use *a lot of* instead of *much* in affirmative sentences.

    Does she wear much makeup?

    No, she doesn't wear much makeup.   OR   Yes, she wears a lot of makeup.

4. Use *any* in negative sentences and questions only.

    Incorrect: I wear any makeup.   He has any tattoos.

    Correct: Do you wear any makeup? No, I don't wear any makeup.

    Does he have any tattoos? No, he doesn't have any tattoos.

5. Do not use *no* in negative sentences.

    Incorrect: I don't wear no makeup.   He doesn't have no tattoos.

    Correct: I wear no makeup.   OR   I don't wear any makeup.

    He has no tattoos.   OR   He doesn't have any tattoos.

6. Sometimes you will see *too* with *much, many, little,* and *few*. The word *too* gives an opinion. It says there is a problem or a complaint. It means the speaker or writer thinks the quantity of something is more than necessary.

    She wears *too much* makeup. He has *too many* tattoos.

    We have *too little* food in the house to make dinner.

    There are *too few* students in class today.

Practice

Activity 1

Circle the indefinite quantifiers and the nouns that follow them. Follow the example.

1. Some people put (a little coloring) in their hair when it becomes gray. Other people don't use any coloring on their gray hair.

2. My friend wears a great deal of makeup. I wear only a little makeup for special occasions. Some people wear no makeup at all.

3. Jenna doesn't wear much perfume. Often she just puts a couple of drops of her favorite perfume behind her ears. Sometimes her husband wears too much cologne.

 Activity 2   (Review sentence patterns in *Destinations 1 Writing for Academic Success—* Unit 1, pp. 8–10 and Unit 2, pp. 39–45.)

In the following journal entries circle the correct word in parentheses.

Monday, March 5
Today in class we learned (many / some) interesting 　　　　　　　　　　　　　　　　　　1
(informations / information) about body decorating. For 　　2
instance, sometimes people spend (a lot of / many) 　　　　　　　　　　　　　　　　　　　3
(time / times) decorating themselves for celebrations. 　4
In this way body art often has (a few / a great deal of) 　　　　　　　　　　　　　　　　　　5
(importance / importances) for (many/much) (people / persons). 　6　　　　　　　　　　7　　　　8
In fact, anthropologists cannot find (any / no) place 　　　　　　　　　　　　　　9
completely without body art or decoration. In some places
people may not have (many / much) permanent body art. 　　　　　　　　　　10
However, they may have at least (a little / a couple of) 　　　　　　　　　　　　　　11
temporary body decoration. In other words, there are (any / no) 　　　　　　　　　　　　　　　　　　　　12
cultures completely without body decoration.

Wednesday, March 7

Today our instructor gave us (a little / a few) specific
1
examples of kinds of body decorating. In (many / much)
2
(society / societies) a person puts (any / some) paint on his or
3   4
her skin. In other places people wear (many / a little) tattoos.
5
If a person has (a few / a great deal of) (wealths / wealth)
6   7
he or she may have a pierced nose decoration. Sometimes a

person's lip plates show (a lot of / a couple of) beauty. Even
8
colors can have (much / many) different meanings. For example,
9
in some places white is a sign of (a great deal of / any) wisdom
10
and understanding. In other places white is a sign of sadness.

Activity 3

Look at these two photos. Write five sentences describing the body art/ decoration you see in these photos. Use one noun and one indefinite quantifier from the lists in each sentence. Be sure to make the count nouns plural if necessary. Use a different noun and quantifier in each of your sentences.

NOUNS:	eye makeup	tattoo	design	pierced ears
	earring	piercing	jewelry	

QUANTIFIERS:	a couple of	a few	several	many
	too much	too many	a great deal of	a little
	much	no	any	too little

1. _____

2. _____

3. _____

4. _____

5. _____

Presentation 2

¹Last night Amira mixed **20 grams of henna powder** with **¼ cup of lemon juice** and covered the mixture to sit overnight. ²This morning she added **2 teaspoons of sugar** and **1 teaspoon of oil** to her henna mixture. ³Now she has **a bowl of henna paste.**

 Questions

1. Look at all the words in bold in these sentences. Circle the last word in bold in each case. Are these words countable or uncountable nouns?

2. What words and expressions tell you how much for each of these nouns? Write these words and expressions on the lines below.

_____   _____   _____

_____   _____

Explanation—Units of Measurement

1. We **cannot** use numbers in front of non-count nouns, but we **can** use units of measure to show more specific or exact quantities. Below are some lists of different units of measure we use with nouns. Most of the nouns on this list are non-count.

Measurements	Containers	Portions	Whole Things
pint/quart/gallon of paint	box of salt	slice of pie	loaf of bread
ounce/liter of water	jar of jam	piece of cheese	head of lettuce
inch/foot/yard of cloth	bag of rice	bowl of cereal	piece of fruit
pound/kilogram/gram of sugar	can of soup	glass of milk	bunch of grapes
hour/minute of time	bottle of juice	cup of tea	bar of soap
tablespoon/teaspoon of powder	carton of eggs		tube of toothpaste

Other: dozen eggs   herd of animals   block of time   drop of syrup

       pile of papers   stick of butter   piece of advice/information/furniture

2. You may use numbers or the articles *a* or *an* (meaning one) before units of measure.

a bag of rice   three bags of rice   an ounce of water   eight ounces of water

(See Lesson 17, page 112 for more information about the articles *a/an*.)

Activity 4

Circle the countable nouns in the units of measurement lists above.

Activity 5

Choose the letter of the best answer for each conversation.

1. How did you wash off all that body paint from your arms and legs?

    a. I used a whole bar of soap.

    b. I used a whole loaf of soap.

2. What kinds of drinks did they serve at the celebration last night?

    a. They had cans of juice and soda.

    b. They had pieces of juice and soda.

3. How much rice do we need for all of our dinner guests?

    a. Please buy one bunch of white rice and a gallon of wild rice.

    b. Please buy one bag of white rice and a box of wild rice.

4. Would you like something to drink?

    a. Thanks, I'll have a bowl of coffee.

    b. Thanks, I'll have a cup of coffee.

5. How much cloth did you use to make that new blouse?

    a. I used two yards of silk.

    b. I used two glasses of silk.

Activity 6

A. *For each number below you will find several units of measure and one noun. Put a line through two units of measure that do not fit each group. Follow the example.*

1. ~~bar of~~	2. gallon of	3. inch of	4. box of	5. pound of
slice of **cake**	pile of	loaf of	bowl of	cup of
~~cup of~~	glass of	piece of	gram of	tablespoon of **butter**
piece of	pound of **water**	foot of **tape**	head of **salt**	stick of
	bottle of	yard of	pound of	head of
	ounce of	meter of	piece of	bag of
		liter of	teaspoon of	

B. *Write a unit of measure in the space provided next to each of the following non-count nouns.*

_____ cotton   _____ oil   _____ mail

_____ dirt   _____ gold   _____ clay

_____ rope   _____ wood   _____ work

Activity 7

A. *On this and the next two pages, you will find pictures of things (nouns). These nouns are in groups according to categories, and the name of each noun is under each picture. Write sentences about these nouns as follows:*

- First, write one sentence about the category.

- Write sentences (a., b., c., etc.) about the nouns in the pictures using different numbers, indefinite quantifiers, and units of measure.

- One of your sentences should also say what you do <u>not</u> see, including the quantifier *no* or *any.* Follow the examples.

EXAMPLE:

Category: fruit

There is a large bowl of fruit.

OR There is a lot of fruit.

OR There is some fruit.

a.   There is a bunch of grapes. OR I see several grapes. OR I see some grapes.

b.   There are no pears in the picture. OR I don't see any pears in the picture.

c.   There are a few strawberries . OR I see three strawberries.

1.

earrings   bracelets   necklace   watches

Category: jewelry

a.   _____

b.   _____

c.   _____

d.   _____

2.

cake   soup   tea   sugar

Category: food

a.   _____

b.   _____

c.   _____

d.   _____

3.

dresses   suit   shirts   jeans

Category: clothing

_____

a. _____

b. _____

c. _____

d. _____

4.

tables

chairs

lamp

Category: furniture

_____

a. _____

b. _____

c. _____

B. *Now think of some celebrations in your country and write some nouns in each of the following categories that you use for those celebrations.*

food: _____

_____

jewelry: _____

_____

clothing: _____

_____

furniture: _____

_____

C. *For each category, write one sentence about using one of the items in B. Use different numbers, indefinite quantifiers, and units of measure in each of your sentences.*

food: _____

_____

jewelry: _____

_____

clothing: _____

_____

furniture: _____

_____

Adjectives

Adjectives/Nouns and Participles as Adjectives

Presentation 1

Questions

1. Look at the words in bold in sentences 1 and 3. What kind of word follows these bold words?

2. Look at the words in bold in sentence 2. What kind of word comes just before these bold words?

3. What kind of information do all of the words in bold give?

[1]People wear many **different** things to show beauty. [2]Sometimes one group's custom is **rare** or seems **strange** to others. [3]This Padaung woman from Thailand is wearing **twenty-four large** rings on her neck.

Explanation—Adjectives

1. Adjectives describe things. They can do this in several ways. They may describe by color, size, general appearance, or other qualities or characteristics.

   People wear many *different* things to show beauty.

   Some customs are *rare*.

2. Adjectives usually come before a noun or after a linking verb.

   (See *Destinations 1 Grammar for Academic Success*, Lessons 9 and 10 for more information about nouns.)
   (See *Destinations 1 Writing for Academic Success*, Unit 2, pp. 39–44 for more information about linking verbs and adjectives.)

   People wear many *different things* to show beauty.
   adjective   noun

Some customs *are rare*.
linking verb adjective

Some customs *seem strange*.
linking verb adjective

Adjectives in English do not add any endings to agree with the nouns. *Do not* add the plural -*s* ending to an adjective.

3. Sometimes we use two or three adjectives to describe a noun. If you use more than one adjective to describe a noun, follow this order:

    NOTE: We usually do not use more than two or three adjectives to describe one noun.

number	opinion	size	shape	age	color	noun
	interesting	small			red	tattoo
	handsome			young		men
two		large	round			bracelets

They met *handsome young* men in that ceremony.

The woman is wearing *two large round* bracelets.

That girl has an *interesting small red* tattoo on her ankle.

4. Some words can make adjectives stronger or weaker. We call these words *qualifiers*. Place these words just before the adjective to give more information about it.

    One group's custom is *fairly rare*.
    qualifier adjective

    Another group's custom is *quite unusual*.
    qualifier adjective

    Some of these words are more common in speaking than in writing. The chart below gives some common examples of qualifiers for adjectives.

    Typical in speech:

    a bit   kind of   sort of   pretty   really   awfully   terribly
    weaker ←————————————————————————————————→ stronger

    Typical in writing:

    hardly   somewhat   almost   rather   fairly   especially   quite   extremely
    weaker ←————————————————————————————————→ stronger

5. The word *very* is also a qualifier. Be careful not to use the word *very* often or to confuse it with *too*. *Very* means much or a large amount. *Too* is more of an opinion. It means the speaker or writer feels there is an amount that is beyond a good amount. (For the use of *too* with quantifiers and nouns see Lesson 11 page 66.)

What is the difference in meaning in the following examples?

Drawing a henna design is *very difficult*.

Drawing a henna design is *too difficult*.

Practice

Activity 1

In the following paragraph, circle all the adjectives and put a line under the qualifiers. Follow the examples.

There is a <u>fairly</u> (small) tribe of people in northern Myanmar (Burma) and Thailand called the Padaung. The women often wear large rings around their necks. By the age of 20, these women often wear five rings. With these rings the necks of these women look quite stretched. In reality, the neck does not become long. The rings are rather heavy, so they push the collarbone down. This custom is old, but nobody remembers the reason for it. Today some women do not want to continue to follow this local tradition.

Activity 2   (Review sentence patterns in *Destinations 1 Writing for Academic Success—*
Unit 1, pp. 8–10 and Unit 2, pp. 39–45.)

You are talking to a friend about a wedding you attended last weekend. Circle the word in parentheses that best fits each sentence. Be prepared to explain your answers.

1. The bride looked (especially / hardly) beautiful in her gown.
2. Also, her new hairstyle was (too / very) different and perfect for the occasion.
3. The groom was (almost / quite) handsome in his tuxedo.
4. The wedding ceremony included (rather / terribly) unusual customs from each of their cultures.
5. It was (very / too) interesting to see these customs.
6. I had a (somewhat / really) good time, and I enjoyed the entire day, but I ate (very / too) much of the delicious food.

Activity 3   (Review sentence patterns in *Destinations 1 Writing for Academic Success*—
Unit 1, pp. 8–10 and Unit 2, pp. 39–45.)

*Fill in the spaces with the adjectives from the list given next to each number
below. Some spaces may have more than one possible answer. Use each
adjective only one time.*

1. *traditional   annual   distant   important   northern   mountainous*

   In _____ _____ Mexico there is a
        a   b

   _____ group of people called Huichol. Corn is especially
      c

   _____ in their lives. They hold _____
      d   e

   ceremonies for planting and harvesting their corn. These rituals started

   in the _____ past, and they continue today.
        f

2. *specific   difficult   similar   bright   typical   yellow*

   Growing food on their land is _____ for the Huichol
                a

   people. Therefore, they developed a system of ceremonies to help bring

   success. As part of their _____ rituals, the Huichol people
              b

   paint their faces with rather _____ designs and patterns.
              c

   They use _____ plants to make sure the paint is
        d

   _____ in color. In this way their patterns are quite
      e

   _____ to pictures of corn.
      f

3. *symbolic   necessary   ceremonial   parallel   complicated*

   Often the _____ designs on their faces are
        a

   _____. They have _____ meaning for the
      b   c

   ritual. For example, _____ lines show the edges of the
            d

   fields of corn. Dots are rows of corn growing in the fields. The Huichol

   believe all these things are extremely _____ for the
                  e

   success of their crops.

Presentation 2

[1]Some people wear **neck rings** as part of their traditions. [2]Other people wear **lip disks**. [3]Many people are **interested** in learning more about these customs. [4]They study these **interesting** customs for different reasons.

Explanation—Nouns and Participles as Adjectives

1. Sometimes a noun describes (modifies) another noun. In this case do not use the *-s* ending.

   Some people wear *neck rings* as part of their traditions.
   　　　　　　　　　　　modifier   noun

   Other people wear *lip disks*.
   　　　　　　　　　modifier   noun

   Usually the words *neck* and *lip* are nouns. In the examples above they are describing (modifying) the nouns *rings* and *disks*.

   Be careful not to use the *-s* ending for noun modifiers of numbers. Look at the following examples:

   It is *a 100-year-old* custom.

   That tattoo cost *five hundred* dollars.

   I paid with a *five dollar* bill.

   NOTE: That custom is *100 years old*.   I will give you *five dollars* for that.

2. A. Sometimes an adjective will have an *-ed* or *-ing* ending. We call these words *participial adjectives*. This is because the *-ing* and *-ed* forms of verbs are called *participles*.

   NOTE: Do not confuse the use of these forms as adjectives with their use as verbs. For more information about verbs with the *-ing* ending, see Lesson 6 (Present Progressive) page 35 and Lesson 32 (Past Progressive) page 230. For more information about *-ed* past participles, see Lessons 34, 35, and 36 (Present Perfect) pages 243–259.

   B. Be careful about using these adjective forms because they have specific meanings. The *-ed* ending describes a feeling or emotion. We often use this ending on adjectives to describe feelings of living things, such as people or animals.

   Correct: John was *bored* at the movie. (The movie was not interesting to John, and this is how he felt.)

   Incorrect: The movie was bored. (A movie does not have feelings.)

The *-ing* ending describes the object that is making someone feel that way. It is the cause or source of a feeling.

> The movie was boring. (The movie was not interesting. It made people feel bored.)

NOTE: It is possible to say *John is boring*. This means John makes other people feel bored. It means his personality is not interesting to other people, and he is the cause (source) of their boredom.

Activity 4

Circle all the noun modifiers in the sentences below.

1. Padaung women wear brass or copper rings on their necks.

2. Padaung women often wear leg and arm bracelets.

3. Another group of people in Thailand put elephant tusks in the women's ears for beauty.

4. Today some Padaung people live in tourist villages in Thailand.

5. We visited these people during our winter break. We will go again for our summer vacation.

Activity 5

A. *For each picture, write the -ed or -ing participle of the adjective on the lines given. Then draw an arrow to show the cause going to the person with the feeling.*

EXAMPLE:

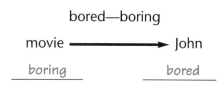

bored—boring

movie ⟶ John

boring   bored

1.   interested—interesting

    Albert   Cynthia

    _____   _____

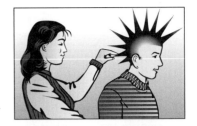

2.   surprised—surprising

    woman   man

    _____   _____

3.   frightened—frightening

    monster   people

    _____   _____

4.   excited—exciting

    clown   child

    _____   _____

Activity 6

Find eight mistakes with adjectives in the following paragraph and show how to correct them. These mistakes may be in the form of the adjective or the word order.

In the Masai tribe of Africa, warriors grow longs hair. They paint their hair with clay red called ochre. They may also wear headdresses of ostriches feathers or a lion's mane. At a certain age, these warriors have a ceremony traditional called Eunoto. This four-days ceremony ends their warriors youth. It puts them into a stage new of life. This is an excited time in these men's lives.

Activity 7   (Review sentence patterns in *Destinations 1 Writing for Academic Success*— Unit 1, pp. 8–10 and Unit 2, pp. 39–45.)

Using the information under each line below, write complete sentences. Be sure to use correct word order, capitalization, and punctuation.

A. _____

usually / is / removable / makeup

_____

some women / such as eyeliner / permanent makeup / these days / get / or eyebrows

B. _____

and dyes / sometimes / important / are / trade items / body paint

_____

of north America / valuable things / Native Americans / for a natural dye / exchanged

C. _____

with vegetable oil / people / natural materials / mix / from plants and minerals

_____

sometimes / also / mix / with animal fat / they / natural materials

_____

body paint / make / different / these mixtures / kinds of

D. _____

of body paints / symbolic / are / colors / often

_____

are / for some people / protective / designs / and body decorations

E. _____

usually / or yellow / is / a clay / red / called ochre

_____

white / some materials / such as chalk / are

_____

skin dyes / to make / leaves / people / from henna and indigo plants / temporary / use

Adjectives

Comparatives and Equatives

¹Marla's smile is **bigger than** Joe's smile.
²Joe's hair is **shorter than** Marla's hair.
³Marla's tattoo is **more detailed than**
Joe's. ⁴They are both wearing dark shirts.
⁵Joe's shirt is **as dark as** Marla's shirt.

Presentation 1—Comparatives

Questions

1. Look at the bold words in sentences 1 and 2. What ending do you see on the adjectives? What information is this ending giving? What word is in bold after the adjective?

2. Look at the bold words in sentence 3. How are these words the same or different from the bold words in sentences 1 and 2?

3. Look at the bold words in sentence 5. What information do these words give?

Explanation—Comparatives and Equatives

1. **Comparatives**—Sometimes we want to compare two people or things to one another. We can do this with adjectives as follows.

    a. Short adjectives—Add the *-er* ending (one syllable or two syllables ending in *-y*).

        Joe's hair is *shorter* than Marla's hair.   Marla seems *happier* than Joe.

        Both Joe and Marla have arm tattoos, but Joe's tattoos are *smaller*.

The following chart shows spelling rules for adjectives when you add the
-*er* ending.

Adjective	Rule	Examples	
Most short adjectives	Add the -*er* ending.	short	short**er**
		small	small**er**
Ends in the letter -*y*	Drop the -*y.* Add -*ier.*	happy	happ**ier**
		dirty	dirt**ier**
Ends in the letter -*e*	Add only the -*r*	large	larg**er**
		brave	brav**er**
Is one syllable and ends in consonant/vowel/consonant	Double the final consonant and add -*er*	big cvc	big**ger**
		hot cvc	hot**ter**

Marla's smile is *bigger* than Joe's smile.

Marla seems *happier* than Joe.

People insert lip disks to make their lips *larger.*

Body art makes warriors look *braver.*

b. Long adjectives—For longer adjectives (two syllables or more) we do not add an ending to the word. Instead, we add the word *more* or the word *less* before the adjective.

Marla's tattoo is more *detailed* than Joe's tattoo.

Joe's tattoo is *less detailed.*

Be careful not to use *more* with an adjective that is already comparative.

INCORRECT: Marla's smile is ~~more~~ bigger than Joe's smile.

NOTE: Some two-syllable words may use either the -*er* ending or the *more . . . than* pattern. Some examples are: *angry, common, friendly, gentle, lively, quiet, simple.*

2. a. When we say both things that we are comparing, we also use the word *than.*

Marla's smile is *bigger than* Joe's smile.

Marla's tattoo is *more detailed than* Joe's tattoo.

NOTE: Be careful to spell *than* correctly. Do not confuse it with the word *then* (for time).

b. Sometimes we may not say the second item in a comparison because we may already understand the meaning. In these cases we may use a possessive, a pronoun, or nothing after the comparison.

(For more information about possessives and pronouns, see Unit 3, Lessons 20 and 21, pages 133–140.)

Marla's smile is *bigger than Joe's smile.*

Marla's smile is *bigger than his.*   Marla's smile is *bigger.*

3. a. The pattern *as + adjective + as* shows that two things are equal or the same. We call this pattern an equative.

Joe's shirt is *as dark as* Marla's shirt.   Your hair is *as short as* mine.

b. We can also make an equative pattern negative to say two things are not the same.

Follow this pattern for negative: *not as + adjective + as.*

His tattoo is *not as big as* her tattoo.

Her tattoo is *not as interesting as* his.

4. Two common adjectives have irregular comparative forms as follows:

good—*better*   bad—*worse*

Practice

Activity 1

Match the first part of the sentence on the left with the correct information on the right. Use each letter only one time. Then circle the comparative or equative in each sentence. Follow the examples.

_C_	1. The Wodaabe men of Niger wear makeup and costumes	a. more attractive than the man next to him.
_h_	2. They use pale yellow powder on their skin	b. when they shave their hairline.
_e_	3. They paint a white line from their forehead to their chin	c. to be (more beautiful) for their Geerewol ceremony.
_d_	4. Their forehead becomes higher	d. than another man for this ceremony.
_g_	5. They walk on their toes during the dance	e. to make their nose look longer.
_a_	6. Each man wants to look	f. the others about this ceremony.
_f_	7. Each man is as serious as	g. to become taller.
_b_	8. No man wants to look less decorative	h. to make it look lighter.

Activity 2   (Review sentence patterns in *Destinations 1 Writing for Academic Success*—
Unit 1, pp. 8–10 and Unit 2, pp. 39–45.)

Comparatives

Fill in the spaces by adding -er *to the adjective given in parentheses or using* the
more + adjective *pattern. Follow the example.*

1. Makeup sometimes makes people feel (young) _____younger_____ .

2. Some people feel tattoos are (protective) __more protective__ than
    other body decorations.

3. In other places body art is (ceremonial) _____ for
    special occasions.

4. In some places body art increases when people become (old)
    _____older_____ .

5. Some societies begin piercings on children (early) ___earlier___
    than in other places.

6. In some places tattoos and piercings are (popular) __more popular__
    with certain kinds of people. Some people may be (rebellious)
    __more rebellious__ than others. In other cases these kinds of
    body art are popular with (spiritual) __more spiritual__ people.
    In other words body art can be (symbolic) __more symbolic__
    than other kinds of decoration for some people.

Equatives

Fill in the spaces by adding as + adjective + as *using the adjective in*
parentheses. Some answers will be negative.

1. Tattoos are (common) __as common as__ pierced ears in some places.

2. That man's hair is (long) __as long as__ his wife's.

3. Your black tattoo is (*negative*–colorful) __not as colorful as__ his
    Irezumi tattoo.

4. Some people wear body decorations to be (fashionable)
    __as fashionable as__ their friends.

5. In some places children are (traditional) __as traditional as__ their
    parents, but in other places they are not.

6. Heavy jewelry is (*negative*–comfortable) __not as comfortable as__ light jewelry
    to wear.

Activity 3

Fill in the spaces with a comparative form of one of the adjectives on the list.
Use each adjective only one time. Be sure to add the word than *when necessary.*
Follow the example.

brave	small	fierce	long	heavy
colorful	large	traditional	successful	

EXAMPLE: Eskimo women added labrets every time they wanted to

make their lips _____larger_____ .

1. Irezumi tattoos are _____ plain black ones.

2. In some places bridal henna is _more traditional than_ in other places. A
     (a)
     friend of the bride's henna designs are _as colorful as_ the designs
     (b)
     on the hands and feet of the bride.

3. Some Native Americans painted their faces to look __longer__
     (a)
     or ___larger___ . They did this to be _more successful_ their
     (b)   (c)
     enemies in battle.   than

4. In Asia some women make their ear lobes ___larger___ by
     (a)
     inserting rings in them. They may do this several times by adding
     __heavier__ rings each time.
     (b)

Activity 4

A. *Find one or two mistakes with comparatives or equatives in most of the*
     following sentences and show how to correct them. One sentence is correct
     and does not need any changes.

1. Gina's leg tattoo is artisticer than her brother's leg tattoo.
     more artistic

2. Bill's more young sister wants to pierce her nose. Bill thinks it's a gooder
     younger   _better_
     idea to wait until she is more older.

3. Pierced ears on men can be as popular pierced ears for women.
                                              _as_

4. Some people wear little or no makeup because they want to have a
     more natural look than a made-up look. Other people feel less
     attractiver without makeup.

B. *Find five mistakes in the following paragraph and show how to correct them.*

More

Gregg is as excited than his wife Judy about getting a new tattoo. Gregg

likes to be different, so his tattoo will have a more unusualer design than

most people's tattoos. Therefore, his tattoo will also be more expensive *than*

Judy's. Judy wants a *more* traditionaler kind of tattoo. Hers will probably be less

expensiver than Gregg's.

Activity 5   (Review sentence patterns in *Destinations 1 Writing for Academic Success—*
Unit 1, pp. 8–10 and Unit 2, pp. 39–45.)

A. *Look at the pictures. Label each sentence below* **T** *for true or* **F** *for false.*
If the sentence is false, rewrite the sentence with correct information. Follow
the example.

EXAMPLE: ___F___ Heidi is taller than Rick.   Rick is taller than Heidi.

___F___ 1. Bob's outfit is more formal than Rick's.

Rick's outfit is more formal than Bob's.

___T___ 2. Heidi's hair is more styled than Lisa's hair.

_____

___F___ 3. Rick's beard is longer than Bob's.

_____

___F___ 4. Lisa's makeup is heavier than Heidi's.

_____

___F___ 5. Heidi is as tall as Rick.

_____

B. *Write your own sentences about these pictures using the adjectives below. Be sure to use a different adjective in each sentence. Write some sentences using a comparative and some sentences using an equative.*

expensive	cheap	fancy	informal
small	large	interesting	happy

1. Heidi's dress is more expensive than Lisa's.
2. Lisa's dress is cheaper than Heidi's.
3. Rich's outfit is more fancy than Bob's.
4. Bob's outfit is more informal than Rich's.
5. Lisa's bague is smaller than Heidi.
6. Rich is larger than Lisa.
7. Heidy is as happy as Rich.
8. Bob and Lisa aren't as interesting as Rich and Heidi.

Activity 6

A. *Write three sentences using comparatives. Use the comparative* less *in at least one sentence.*

1. My shoes are less expensive than yours.
2. The book is as big as his bag.
3. Jane loves cats more than dogs.

B. *Write two sentences using equatives.*

1. _____
2. _____

Adjectives

Superlatives

[1]The *Guinness World Records* website includes many of **the most extraordinary** facts about things on this planet. [2]For example, they have information about everything from **the world's tallest** man ever on record (8 ft 11.1 in/236 cm) to **the world's shortest** living man (Younis Edwan of Jordan—25.5 in/65 cm). [3]They also include records such as **the most valuable** jewelry collection ($50,427,977 paid in 1997) and **the most decorated** bodies of men and women around the world.

Presentation—Superlatives

Questions

1. Look at the adjectives in bold in sentence 2. What ending do you see on these words? What information does this ending give? What word comes before these adjectives?

2. Look at the adjectives in bold in sentences 1 and 3. What two words come before each of those adjectives?

Explanation—Superlatives

1. In Lesson 13 you learned about using adjectives to compare two things (comparatives) and to show how two things are the same (equatives).

   We can also use adjectives to show that something is the top or bottom of a group of things (more than two things). We call these *superlatives*.

2. **Short adjectives**—Add the -*est* ending for short adjectives. We also add the definite article *the* before these forms.

   The *Guiness World Records* website has information about everything from *the tallest* living woman to *the shortest* living man.

   The largest garlic festival in the world takes place every summer in the town of Gilroy, California. *The biggest* religious feast took place in India in 1991 (150,000 guests).

The chart below shows spelling rules for adjectives when you add the -est ending.

Adjective	Rule	Examples	
Most short adjectives	Add the -est ending.	short	short**est**
		tall	tall**est**
Ends in the letter -y	Drop the -y. Add -iest.	happy	happ**iest**
		dirty	dirt**iest**
Ends in the letter -e	Add only the -st	large	larg**est**
		brave	brav**est**
Is one syllable and ends in consonant/vowel/consonant	Double the final consonant and add -est	big CVC	big**gest**
		hot CVC	hot**test**

3. **Long adjectives**—For longer adjectives we do not add an ending to the word. Instead, we add the word *most* before the adjective for the largest amount. For the smallest amount, we use *least* for non-count nouns or *fewest* for count nouns. We also add the definite article *the* before these forms.

> The *Guinness World Records* include many of *the most extraordinary* facts about things on this planet. They have some records of things at the bottom of a group, such as the language with *the fewest* vowel sounds (2) or a book with *the least information* (52 blank pages).

4. Two common adjectives have irregular superlative forms as follows:

> good—*best*   bad—*worst*

Practice

Activity 1

Put the letter of the correct Guinness World Record *about body art/decoration on the space next to each number.*

_____ 1. the longest neck

a. Shamsher Singh of India—6ft (1.83 cm) long

_____ 2. the largest lip plates

b. women in Southeast Asia wearing heavy rings

_____ 3. the most tattooed men

c. 15.75 in (40 cm) on a Padaung woman

_____ 4. the longest beard

d. a woman with 192 on ears, forehead, and eyebrows

_____ 5. the most elongated ear lobes

e. up to 6 in (15 cm) on Surma women in Ethiopia

_____ 6. the most decorated face of piercings

f. two men with 99.9% of their bodies covered

Activity 2

A. *The following facts about language are missing a superlative. Can you guess the correct information for each one? Fill in a superlative from the list for each blank space. Use each one only one time. The correct answers are at the end of this lesson.*

a. rarest	b. largest	c. most complicated
d. most widespread	e. oldest	f. most common

1. The _____ language in the world is Chinese with more than 900 million speakers.

2. The _____ language in the world is English, so you can speak English in many places.

3. Inuit is one of the _____ languages in the world. It has 63 forms of the present tense.

4. One of the _____ sounds in the world is the click from the Kalahari Bushman language "!xo".

5. The _____ letter may be "O" because it hasn't changed its shape since the Phoenician alphabet written 3000 years ago.

6. The language with the _____ number of irregular verbs is English (283 verbs).

B. *Choose the superlative to fit each fact about marriages and weddings from the* Guinness World Records *website. Write the letter of your answer in the space of the sentence it fits. The correct answers are at the end of this lesson.*

(Review sentence patterns in *Destinations 1 Writing for Academic Success*—Unit 1, pp. 8–10 and Unit 2, pp. 39–45.)

a. the highest divorce rate	b. the longest marriage
c. the lowest marriage rate	d. the oldest bride
e. the largest number of bridesmaids and groomsmen	

1. _____ was a 102-year-old Australian woman named Minnie Munaro.

2. In 2005 Percy and Florence Arrowsmith of the United Kingdom had _____ of a living couple (81 years).

3. The Maldives Islands have _____ with 10.97 divorces per 1,000 people.

4. In 1994 (the last year of available records) _____ was in the Dominican Republic with two marriages per 1,000 people.

5. The wedding with _____ took place in Ontario, Canada in September of 2003. (79 bridesmaids, ages one to 79 and 47 groomsmen ages two to 63).

Activity 3

Write the superlative for each of the adjectives given. When you see (-), you should use the superlative to show the smallest amount. Be sure to include the word the *with each superlative.*

1. She has _____ tattoo on her shoulder.
   _{unusual}

2. That new tattoo is _____ of all of your body art.
   _{attractive (-)}

3. The colors on the flower tattoo are _____ of all your tattoos.
   _{bright}

4. The tiny flower on her ankle is _____ tattoo on her body.
   _{small}

5. Having several piercings on my face is _____ body decoration to me.
   _{appealing (-)}

6. My friend likes to look different, so she always gets _____ kind of body art.
   _{strange}

7. You have _____ eyes even without any makeup.
   _{beautiful}

Activity 4

Find eight mistakes with superlatives and equatives. Show how to correct each one.

Betty, Phyllis, and Gina are all very good friends with different ideas about fashion.

1. Betty is most modern-thinking. She wears only the most newest styles of makeup and clothes. She is always the bestest dressed of the three friends.

2. Phyllis is the old-fashionedest and conservative. She doesn't like latest styles or most unusual fashions.

3. Gina isn't as financially secure her friends. She likes the new styles, but she is the leastest able to afford anything expensive. She always looks for the biggest bargains in the stores.

Activity 5   (Review sentence patterns in *Destinations 1 Writing for Academic Success*—
Unit 1, pp. 8–10 and Unit 2, pp. 39–45.)

*Write two sentences about each person in these pictures. Your sentences should
describe how these people look. Include some information about them from the
pictures. In each sentence use a superlative of one of the adjectives in the list
below. Be sure to use* the most, the least *and the -est ending in your sentences.*

Steve	Barbara	Carla
$600—three tattoos	$20 per piercing	$200—makeup

Adjectives:	old	inexpensive	cheap	unattractive	decorative
	nice	expensive	young	appealing	interesting

Steve: _____

_____

_____

Barbara: _____

_____

_____

Carla: _____

_____

_____

Activity 6

What are your opinions about tattoos, piercings on the face, and makeup?
Write one or two sentences about each of these subjects using the superlative of
one of the following words in each of your sentences. Be sure to use the most,
the least *or* the fewest, *and the -est ending in your sentences.*

ADJECTIVES: pretty   attractive   easy   uncomfortable   surprising
strange   unappealing   simple   interesting   difficult

EXAMPLE: Piercings on the face are *the most unusual* kinds of body art.

_____

_____

_____

_____

_____

_____

_____

Answers to Activity 2 on pages 93–94:

A. 1. f   2. d   3. c   4. a   5. e   6. b

B. 1. d   2. b   3. a   4. c   5. e

Prepositions

Prepositions of Location: Time

[1]In the United States there are several holidays and big celebrations **in December.** [2]For example, many people have New Year's Eve parties **on December 31.** [3]They celebrate **for several hours before New Year's Day** begins officially **at midnight.**

Presentation

Questions

1. Look at the words in bold in sentence 1. Which word is a preposition? What kind of information follows this preposition?

2. Look at the words in bold in sentence 2. Which word is a preposition? What kind of information follows this preposition?

3. Circle the prepositions in bold in sentence 3. What does each of these words mean?

Explanation—Prepositions of Location: Time

1. There are many *prepositions* in English, such as *in, at, on, to, from,* etc. These words connect nouns and pronouns to other parts of a sentence.

   Prepositions and the words after them are called *prepositional phrases.*

   > Many people have New Year's Eve parties *on* December 31.
   >   preposition

   > Many people have New Year's Eve parties *on December 31.*
   >   prepositional phrase

2. Prepositions can tell the relationship between a noun or pronoun and the rest of the sentence. However, prepositions are not usually necessary to show a noun or pronoun is a subject or object of a sentence.

   In this lesson you will learn about prepositions that show location in time.

   > Many people have New Year's Eve parties *on December 31.*
   >   subject   object   prepositional phrase (time relationship)

   > They celebrate *for several hours.*
   > subject   prepositional phrase (time relationship)

3. Sometimes prepositional phrases can move around in a sentence.

    Many people have New Year's Eve parties *on December 31*.

    On December 31 many people have New Year's Eve parties.

4. Two common prepositions of time are *from* and *to*.

    From tells you the **beginning** time and *to* tells you the **end** time.

    We were at the New Year's Eve party last night *from* 8 p.m. *to* midnight.
    beginning   end

5. *In, on,* and *at* are three other common prepositions of time. Often *at* is the most specific and *in* is the most general of these.

    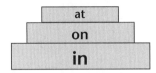

    New Year's Day begins *at 12 midnight*. (exact/specific time)

    This year New Year's Eve is *on Wednesday*. (day of the week)

    New Year's Eve is *on December 31*. (date)

    In the evening* I'll help my friend prepare her party. (time of day)

    New Year's Eve is *in December*. (month)

    There are many holidays *in the winter*. (time of year)

    The best New Year's Eve party was *in 2006*. (year)

    *We say *in the morning, in the afternoon, in the evening,* but *at night*.

6. *Before, after, during, between* and *for* are other prepositions of time.

    before = earlier than

    Before the holiday we will buy new clothes.

    after = later than

    After the celebration I'll take off my makeup.

    during = throughout that time/in the time of

    I'll talk to you *during* the party.

    between = within two limits of time

    You should arrive at the party *between* 8:00 and 9:00 p.m.

    for† = amount of time/how much time

    We stayed at the celebration *for three hours* last night.

    †You will often find *for* with an amount of time in sentences using present perfect verbs. See Unit 6, Lesson 35, page 252 for more information about this use of *for*.

Practice

Activity 1

Circle the prepositions of time in the following sentences.

1. The Vietnamese New Year (Tet) starts during the full moon before spring planting.

2. Chinese people celebrate from the first day to the 15th day of their new year.

3. U.S. Thanksgiving always takes place on the last Thursday in November.

4. The Thai Loy Kratong Festival happens at night in the twelfth lunar month.

5. Persian Nowruz starts at the beginning of spring and lasts for 13 days.

6. The Korean New Year (Shul) occurs on the first day in the first month on a lunar calendar.

Activity 2

Circle the correct preposition in parentheses in this student's journal entry.

Thursday, March 5
(In / On) Monday in my Cultural Anthropology 152 class, we   1
discussed body decoration and special celebrations. Fahin told
us about the bridal henna party that she had (in / on)
December. She explained this celebration could take place   2
(from / to) one (from / to) several days (between / before) a   3   4   5
wedding. Her party took place (after / during) the arrival of her   6
out-of-town relatives.
(During / From) her party her cousin painted henna designs on   7
her hands and feet. She left the henna paste on her skin (for / in)   8
a long time, and (at / in) the evening it became a dark color.   9
(On / At) the end of the day, these temporary designs were   10
still on her skin.

W   *Activity 3*   (Review sentence patterns in *Destinations 1 Writing for Academic Success*—
Unit 1, pp. 8–10 and Unit 2, pp. 39–45.)

A.   *Fill in the spaces with one of the four prepositions listed below. You will need
to use each preposition two times.*

for	at	from	to

1.   Surma women in Ethiopia wear lip plates _____ childhood

_____ adulthood.

2.   Irezumi artists may work _____ many hours on one tattoo.

3.   In the Tchikrin tribe of the Amazon, a boy stops living with his mother

_____ eight years old.

4.   Wodaabe men hold an important celebration called Geerewol

_____ several days each year.

5.   In some tribes fathers pierce the earlobes of their babies _____

birth.

6.   Aborigines in Australia pass body decoration designs _____ one

generation _____ another.

B.   *Fill in the spaces with one of the prepositions listed below. Use each
preposition only one time.*

at	for	during	in	before	between	on

1.   The Vietnamese Tet holiday usually occurs _____ January or

February on the Western calendar.

2.   The Tet celebration can take place _____ almost a week.

3.   _____ this holiday people prepare for it by buying new

clothes and presents to give to friends and family.

4.   Giao Thua is one of the most important times _____ the

Tet holidays. It occurs _____ midnight _____

New Year's Eve. It is the time _____ the old year and

the new.

Activity 4

Each preposition in bold below is incorrect. Correct each one using prepositions from the list below. Use each preposition on the list only one time.

from	to	before	at	during	on	after	in

On the Eunoto ceremony of the Masai tribe in Africa, the warrior men wear red ochre body paint. **At** the second day of the ceremony, they paint their bodies with chalk designs. **To** another part of the ceremony, each man's mother scrapes off his hair **in** sunrise. This shows the men are moving **to** the warrior stage of their life **from** a mature age. **After** this Eunoto ceremony a young man is a warrior, but **before** this time he is more like a tribal elder.

Activity 5   (Review sentence patterns in *Destinations 1 Writing for Academic Success—* Unit 1, pp. 8–10 and Unit 2, pp. 39–45.)

Look at the calendars on this page and the next page. Use the information about the holidays on these calendars to write sentences of your own. Use at least one preposition of time from the list below in each sentence. Use each preposition on the list at least one time.

Prepositions: in	on	before	after	from	to	during	between

NOVEMBER 2007

Sunday	Monday	Tuesday	Wednesday	Thursday	Friday	Saturday
				1	2	3
4	5	6	7	8	9	10
11	12	13	14	15	16	17
18	19	20	21	22	23	24
25	26	27	28	29	30	

Thanksgiving, November 22, 2007

EXAMPLES:

In 2007, Thanksgiving in the United States was on Thursday, November 22.

In 2007, Thanksgiving in the United States came several months after the Chinese and Persian New Year holidays.

JANUARY 2007

Sunday	Monday	Tuesday	Wednesday	Thursday	Friday	Saturday
	1	2	3	4	5	6
7	8	9	10	11	12	13
14	15	16	17	18	19	20
21	22	23	24	25	26	27
28	29	30	31			

1.   Western New Year   New Year's Day, Western Calendar, Year 2007

_____

_____

FEBRUARY 2007

Sunday	Monday	Tuesday	Wednesday	Thursday	Friday	Saturday
				1	2	3
4	5	6	7	8	9	10
11	12	13	14	15	16	17
18	19	20	21	22	23	24
25	26	27	28			

2.   Chinese New Year   Chinese New Year, Year of the Pig, Year 4705

_____

_____

MARCH 2007

Sunday	Monday	Tuesday	Wednesday	Thursday	Friday	Saturday
				1	2	3
4	5	6	7	8	9	10
11	12	13	14	15	16	17
18	19	20	21	22	23	24
25	26	27	28	29	30	31

3.   Persian New Year—Nowruz   Persian New Year of Nowruz, Year 1386

_____

_____

Prepositions

Prepositions of Location: Place

[1]Gerry traveled **from** his home state of New York **to** many countries **in** Asia and the Pacific Ocean. [2]He saw people **in** different countries and **on** different islands wearing several kinds of body decorations. [3]The most interesting kinds were **at** special celebrations.

Presentation 1

Questions

1. What do you think the prepositions *from* and *to* mean in sentence 1?

2. In sentences 1 and 2 find the preposition *in*. What nouns come after these prepositions?

3. In sentence 2 what noun comes after the preposition *on*?

4. What noun comes after the preposition *at* in sentence 3?

Explanation 1—Prepositions of Place
(*in / at / on / to / from / between / near / next to*)

1. As discussed in Lesson 15, prepositions give information about the nouns and pronouns in a sentence. In this lesson you will learn about prepositions of place.

2. Two common prepositions of place are *from* and *to*.

   From tells you the **beginning** place (the source).

   To tells you the **end** place.

   > Gerry traveled *from* his home state of New York *to* many countries.
   >   beginning   end

3. *In, on,* and *at* are three other common prepositions of place. Often *at* is the most specific and *in* is the most general.

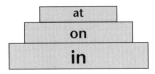

She lives **at 356 Oak Street.** (specific address)

I saw her **at the New Year's Eve party at the Grant Hotel.** (specific places)

She lives **on College Avenue.** (street name)

He lives **in San Diego.** (city)

He lives **in California.** (state)

He lives **in the United States.** (country)

She lives **in Asia.** (larger area)

4. We also sometimes use *in* and *on* for the following meanings:

   a. *in* = inside

      The New Year's Eve party was *in* a large hotel.

      on = on top of/the surface

      He put his glass of juice *on* the table.

   b. Sometimes you will use these prepositions with specific kinds of transportation as follows:

      in   car/taxi

      He is riding *in* a taxi to get to his hotel.

      on   airplane/train/bus/motorcycle/bicycle

      The passengers are all *on* the airplane now.

5. *Between, near,* and *next to* are other prepositions of place.

   between = within two places

   The Hawaiian Islands are in the Pacific Ocean *between* North America and Asia.

   near = close to; not far

   The islands of the Philippines are *near* the islands of Indonesia in the Pacific Ocean.

   next to = closest to/beside

   Portugal is *next to* Spain on the Iberian Peninsula.

Practice

Activity 1

Complete each sentence (1–6) using the best prepositional phrase (a–f). Some answers may fit more than one sentence, but you should use each answer only one time. Also, circle each preposition of place in all of the sentences.

_____ 1. In the Amazon an eight-year-old boy moves from his mother's hut

_____ 2. Some people put paint from the Urucu plant

_____ 3. At the Geerowol celebration in Niger, Woodaabe men stand

_____ 4. On special holidays people often travel large distances to be

_____ 5. Some people wear special decorations

_____ 6. People use sharp objects to insert piercings

a. between their eyebrows.

b. next to each other and dance.

c. on their bodies at celebrations.

d. in their ears and lips.

e. near their families.

f. to a man's hut to live.

Activity 2   (Review sentence patterns in *Destinations 1 Writing for Academic Success*—Unit 1, pp. 8–10 and Unit 2, pp. 39–45.)

Circle the correct preposition in each set of parentheses in the following paragraph.

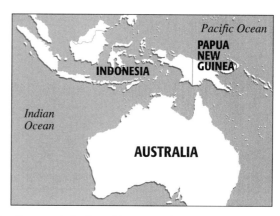

Papua New Guinea is an island (in / on) the Pacific Ocean. It is (on / between)
　　　　　　　　　　　　　　　　　　　1　　　　　　　　　　　　　　　　　2

Australia and many small Pacific Islands called Micronesia. Papua New Guinea

is (in / on) the same island as one part of Indonesia. Therefore, it is
　　3

(next to / between) one part of Indonesia. This means you can travel
　　4

(at / from) Papua New Guinea (to / in) this part of Indonesia without
　　5　　　　　　　　　　　　　　6

crossing any water. Papua New Guinea is also (near / in) Australia. However,
　　　　　　　　　　　　　　　　　　　　　　　　　　　7

to travel (at / from) Papua New Guinea (to / in) Australia, you must cross a
　　　　　8　　　　　　　　　　　　　　9

body of water.

Activity 3

A man is traveling to be with his family for a special holiday. He is at the airport now, and a customs officer is looking at his papers. Read the information on this man's papers and complete the activity that follows.

Name:	*George Abbas*
Place of Birth:	*Toronto, Canada*
Nationality:	*Canadian*
Originating Airport:	*Chicago, O'Hare Airport*
Final Destination:	*Cairo, Egypt*
Permanent Address:	*7355 Mt. Vernon St.*
	Detroit, Michigan, U.S.A.
Local Address:	*100 El Orouba Street*
	Cairo, Egypt

A. Fill in the blanks with the correct information from above after each preposition. More than one answer may be possible in some of the spaces. Use each piece of information only one time.

Cairo	Toronto	Mt. Vernon St.	the United States
Egypt	O'Hare Airport	100 El Orouba Street	Cairo Airport
Michigan	Detroit	his brother's house	El Orouba Street

George Abbas is a traveler from _____ . He was born in
                                          1

_____ , but now he lives in _____ on
        2   3

_____ . He flew this morning from _____ to
        4   5

_____ . He will stay in _____ for one week at
        6   7

_____ . His brother lives on _____ at
        8   9

_____ . After he spends one week in _____ , he
        10   11

will go home to _____ .
                        12

B. *Do this part with a partner.*

• Tell your partner about where you live now by completing the following sentences.

I live in _____. My apartment/house/dormitory is on

_____. I live at _____.

• Now tell your partner where you lived in the past by completing the same sentences.

I lived in _____. My apartment/house/dormitory was on

_____. I lived at _____.

• Together with your partner describe the location of your school using the same sentences from above.

_____

_____

_____

_____

_____

_____

Presentation 2

[1]For some holidays people make parades **through** the streets. [2]Some people may walk **behind** an important symbol of the holiday, such as a dragon. [3]Other people may walk **under** a dragon to move it in the parade. [4]They hold the dragon **over** their heads during the parade.

Explanation 2—Prepositions of Place
(*behind / in front of / under / over / above / below / across / through / around*)

1. In Explanation 1 you learned several prepositions of place and direction. In Explanation 2 there are a few more as follows:

    behind = at the back of something

    > In a parade some people may walk *behind* an important symbol.

    in front of = in a position ahead of something

    > Sometimes the most important people walk *in front of* the others in a parade.

    under = lower than (a position lower than)

    > People may walk *under* a dragon to move it in the parade.

    over = higher than (in a position higher than)

    > Some men held the dragon *over* their heads during the parade.

    above = directly higher than something

    > Sometimes people show fireworks *above* the crowds at a celebration.

    below = directly lower than something

    > The people *below* the fireworks look at the sky to see the show.

    across = from one side to another/on the other side

    > We walked *across* the street to get a better view of the fireworks.

    through = from one end to another/in one side and out another

    > For some holidays people make parades *through* the streets.

    around = surrounding/encircling

    > At some celebrations people may dance *around* a fire.

Activity 4

A. *The following sentences describe the pictures of Aboriginal art below. Circle all the prepositions of place in these sentences.*

1. Women are sitting around a campsite or fire.

2. Two men are sitting across a campsite or fire.

3. The rain is falling to the earth below the sky.

4. We can see a star above the earth.

5. Water is running through this area from one waterhole

    to another.

B. *Fill in the spaces of the following paragraph about the Aboriginal symbols with one of the prepositions from the list. Use each preposition only one time.*

to	on	in	from

Aboriginal people _____ the deserts of Australia use stripes
                           1

and circles as symbols for their drawings. They paint these pictures

_____ their bodies and faces. These paintings tell important
        2

stories, so the people pass these decorations _____ one
                                                        3

generation _____ another.
                   4

Activity 5

Circle the correct preposition in parentheses in the following paragraph.

Last year I went (from / to) a New Year's Eve party (at / on) my friend's
⠀⠀⠀⠀⠀⠀⠀⠀⠀⠀⠀1⠀⠀⠀⠀⠀⠀⠀⠀⠀⠀⠀⠀⠀⠀⠀⠀⠀⠀2

apartment (on / in) New York City. My friend lives (on / in) a building
⠀⠀⠀⠀⠀⠀⠀3⠀⠀⠀⠀⠀⠀⠀⠀⠀⠀⠀⠀⠀⠀⠀⠀⠀⠀⠀⠀⠀⠀⠀⠀4

(on / in) 88th Street. More specifically, she lives (on / at) 37-05 88th St.
⠀5⠀⠀⠀⠀⠀⠀⠀⠀⠀⠀⠀⠀⠀⠀⠀⠀⠀⠀⠀⠀⠀⠀⠀⠀⠀⠀⠀6

To get to the party, I took a subway (to / from) my hotel (to / from) her
⠀⠀⠀⠀⠀⠀⠀⠀⠀⠀⠀⠀⠀⠀⠀⠀⠀⠀⠀⠀7⠀⠀⠀⠀⠀⠀⠀⠀⠀⠀8

neighborhood. At first the subway traveled (near / below) the street. Then it
⠀⠀⠀⠀⠀⠀⠀⠀⠀⠀⠀⠀⠀⠀⠀⠀⠀⠀⠀⠀⠀⠀⠀⠀⠀⠀9

took us (through / between) a tunnel (between / under) a river. We also
⠀⠀⠀⠀⠀⠀⠀10⠀⠀⠀⠀⠀⠀⠀⠀⠀⠀⠀⠀⠀11

went (across / above) the ground for a while, and we could see the busy
⠀⠀⠀⠀⠀12

streets. I tried to walk (from / near) the subway station (through / to) my
⠀⠀⠀⠀⠀⠀⠀⠀⠀⠀⠀⠀⠀⠀13⠀⠀⠀⠀⠀⠀⠀⠀⠀⠀⠀⠀⠀⠀14

friend's apartment, but I got lost. Then I walked (between / around) her
⠀⠀⠀⠀⠀⠀⠀⠀⠀⠀⠀⠀⠀⠀⠀⠀⠀⠀⠀⠀⠀⠀⠀⠀⠀⠀⠀⠀⠀15

neighborhood for a few minutes. Finally, I found her building. It was right

(across / in) the street from the subway station!
⠀16

 Activity 6⠀⠀(Review sentence patterns in *Destinations 1 Writing for Academic Success—*
⠀⠀⠀⠀⠀⠀⠀⠀⠀⠀⠀⠀⠀⠀Unit 1, pp. 8–10 and Unit 2, pp. 39–45.)

 *All the prepositions in bold in the paragraphs below are incorrect. Correct each
one using a preposition from the list above each paragraph. For each paragraph
you will use one preposition on the list two times. You will use all the other
prepositions on each list only once.*

for	around	on	in	at	over

A.⠀Nowruz is an important holiday **at** Persian countries. In fact, Persian
⠀⠀people **on** the world celebrate this New Year's holiday. It starts **for** the
⠀⠀beginning of spring and continues **in** 13 days. **Over** the last Tuesday
⠀⠀night of the old year, people gather **on** bonfires. As part of this ritual,
⠀⠀they jump **under** fires to clean their body of bad things and pick up the
⠀⠀warmth of the fire.

during	through	on	to	around	from

B. **Over** the first day of spring, families sit **above** a table set with an
arrangement of seven important items. Also **under** this holiday some
men wear makeup and brightly colored clothes. These men, called Haji
Faruz, sing and dance **at** the streets. Then **at** the final day of the holiday
some people go **on** their homes **below** the countryside for a picnic.

Activity 7

*Look at the photograph of a woman with
several kinds of body decorations. Write five
sentences to describe these decorations using
at least one of the following prepositions in
each sentence.*

in	on	at	between	to	from
over	below	above	under	through	

1. _____

2. _____

3. _____

4. _____

5. _____

Articles

Indefinite Articles (*A/An*) and Definite Article (*The*)

[1]Hernan Cortés was **a conquistador.** [2]He came to Mexico in 1519 to find **some gold** and other valuable materials. [3]He found **an interesting civilization** of native people living there, called Aztecs. [4]These Aztec people had **a ruler,** and his name was Moctezuma.

Presentation 1

Questions

1. Circle all the countable nouns in bold in these four sentences.

2. Put a line under the one non-count noun in bold. Then put a line under the indefinite quantifier in bold with this non-count noun.

3. Look at the two bold words in sentence 4. Is the noun singular or plural? What kind of word comes before it?

4. Look at the bold words in sentence 3 and sentence 4. Why is the first word in bold different in these two sentences?

Explanation—Indefinite Article: *A/An*

1. In Lessons 9, 10, and 11, you learned about nouns and quantifiers. Count nouns can be singular or plural, but non-count nouns have only one form. Indefinite quantifiers may come before nouns.
   (See Unit 2, pp. 53–66 for a review of this information.)

   The Aztec people had *one ruler*.
         count noun (singular)

   They did not have *several rulers*.
         quantifier—count noun (plural)

   Cortés wanted to find *some gold*.
         quantifier—non-count noun

2. We often use the words *a* or *an* with a singular countable noun. We call *a/an indefinite articles.* Use of *a/an* means there is only one of this item. It also means this noun is not specific but more general.

   We use the indefinite article when the listener or speaker is not familiar with or doesn't know the noun we are talking about. We also use the indefinite article to say that something is one of a group.

   Hernan Cortés was *a conquistador.*   The Aztec people had *a ruler.*

3. We use the *an* form of the indefinite article when the following word has a vowel **sound.** This word may be a noun or another word, such as an adjective. (vowels = a, e, i, o, u)

   Cortés was *a conquistador* from Spain.
   _{noun—consonant **sound**}

   He met with **an** *Aztec* named Moctezuma.
   noun—vowel sound

   Cortés found **an** *interesting civilization* of native people.
   adjective—vowel sound

   REMEMBER: The *an* goes before a vowel **sound.** Sometimes you will find *an* before a consonant because it has a vowel sound *(an honor/ an honest person)*, and *a* before a vowel because it has a consonant sound *(a university).*

4. **IMPORTANT:** We use indefinite articles *(a/an)* for singular count nouns ONLY. **Do not** use indefinite articles with non-count nouns or with plural nouns. It may be helpful to think of an indefinite article as the number *one.*

   Cortés was *a soldier* (one soldier), and he rode *a horse* (one horse).

Practice

Activity 1

Fill in the chart on the next page with words from the story as follows:

A. *Write each indefinite article* (a/an) *and the singular count noun following it in the column on the left.*

B. *Write each indefinite quantifier and the non-count noun after it in the column on the right. If there is an adjective before the noun, write that word as well. Follow the examples in the chart.*

Cortés found Native Americans living in a city called Tenochtitlán. This city was on an island in the middle of a lake. These people developed an

on water advanced system of agriculture. They built *floating* islands in order to grow a great deal of food for a large population. To make an *artificial* island, they   man-made/ not natural

put branches and reeds from plants in some lake water. Then they placed some mud on these small rafts. In this way they made a lot of rich earth to grow lots of food, such as corn, beans, and tomatoes.

A	B
a city	a great deal of food

Activity 2

Circle the indefinite article in parentheses for each noun in both Column A and column B. Then put the letter of the meaning or description from Column B in the space next to each number in A. Follow the example.

A

___i___ 1. ((a)/ an) conquistador

_____ 2. (a / an) European

_____ 3. (a / an) Aztec

_____ 4. (a / an) century

_____ 5. (a / an) mestizo

_____ 6. (a / an) ancestor

_____ 7. (a / an) inhabitant

_____ 8. (a / an) immigrant

_____ 9. (a / an) journey

_____ 10. (a / an) ocean

_____ 11. (a / an) treaty

_____ 12. (a / an) colony

B

a. (a / an) period of 100 years

b. (a / an) relative who came before you

c. (a / an) trip

d. (a / an) mixture of European and Indian

e. (a / an) permanent resident of a place

f. (a / an) large body of water

g. (a / an) area subject to rule by another country

h. (a / an) agreement

i. ((a)/ an) Spanish soldier

j. (a / an) Italian or (a / an) Spaniard

k. (a / an) Native American

l. (a / an) person who comes to a new country to live

W **Activity 3** (Review coordinating conjunctions in *Destinations 1 Writing for Academic Success*—Unit 3, pp. 66–75.)

A. *Fill in the spaces of the following paragraph using* a, an, any, *or* some. *Then circle the noun following each article or quantifier you wrote.*

_____ Aztec city always had _____ marketplace.
         1   2
However, Aztec people did not use _____ money, so they traded
                                                        3

or made exchanges for things. In _____ Aztec marketplace a

person could get _____ clothing, food, or jewelry. For example,

_____ person could buy _____ finger ring or

_____ plug for _____ pierced lip.

B. *Fill in the spaces of the following paragraph using* a, an, some, *or* much.

The Aztecs of Tenochtitlán lived in the middle of _____ lake, but

they needed _____ agricultural system and _____ fresh

supply of water for drinking. This is because their lake had too

_____ salt, so they could not drink it. They developed

_____ way to bring fresh water from _____ underground

spring. This spring was three miles away, so they built _____

aqueduct to carry the water. They made their aqueduct by putting

_____ wood and stones in lines to make _____ long

channel to carry the water.

[1]The Spaniards colonized **a large area** of land, and they called **the area** New Spain. [2]**The Spanish armies** destroyed Tenochtitlán and built **a new city** in its place. [3]**The new city** (Mexico City) became **the capital** of **the Spanish colony.**

Presentation 2

Questions

1. Circle the article and noun in the first group of bold words in sentence 1. Do we know the specific colonized area from these words?

2. Circle the noun in the second group of bold words in sentence 1. What word comes before this noun? Why do we use *the* and not *a* in this case?

3. Circle the article and noun in the second group of bold words in sentence 2. Do we know anything specific about the noun *city?*

4. Why is the article *the* in each of the bold group of words in sentence 3?

Explanation—Definite Article: *The*

1. As discussed in Presentation 1 of this lesson, we use the articles *a/an* with a singular noun when it is indefinite or not specific.

   The Spaniards colonized *a large area of land.*

   They destroyed Tenochtitlán and built *a new city.*

2. We use the definite article *the* for specific nouns. This means the reader or listener knows about the item. It is clear who or what the speaker or writer is talking/writing about.

   The conquistador Cortés conquered *the Aztecs.*

   The Spaniards built Mexico City.

   We also use *the* when there is only one of something, so we know exactly what it is.

   The Aztecs worshipped *the sun.* (There is only one sun.)

   Mexico City became *the capital* of New Spain.
   (There is only one capital city.)

3. Use the definite article *the* with all of the following when the noun is specific:

   a. A singular count noun

      The new city (Mexico City) became *the capital of the colony.*

   b. Plural count nouns

      The Spanish armies destroyed Tenochtitlán.

      The conquistadors conquered *the Aztec people.*

   c. Non-count nouns

      The agriculture of the Aztecs surprised the conquistadors.

      The Spaniards also saw *the courage* of the Aztec people.

4. We use an indefinite article when we are talking about something for the first time. When we mention this item again, we use the definite article because we already know about it.

   The Spaniards colonized *a large area* of land, and they called *the area* New Spain.

   The Spaniards built *a new city,* and *the new city* became Mexico City.

5. As discussed in Lesson 14 (page 91), we use *the* with superlatives. We also use *the* when we mention the order of things, such as *the first, the second, the next,* etc.

   Tenotchtitlán was *the biggest* city of the Aztecs. Cortés and his men *were the first Spaniards* to meet Moctezuma.

6. We do not use the definite article *the* with most names of cities, states, and countries.

> Cortés came from Spain to Mexico. The Spaniards destroyed Tenochtitlán and built Mexico City.

NOTE: There are a few countries (with plural names) that use the definite article as follows:

the United States	*the* Philippines
the United Kingdom	*the* Netherlands

Activity 4   (Review coordinating conjunctions in *Destinations 1 Writing for Academic Success*—Unit 3, pp. 66–75.)

A. *In the paragraph below put a line under the indefinite articles* (a/an) *and circle the definite articles* (the).

B. *Then answer the questions that follow T for True and F for False about the information.*

¹A granddaughter of Cortés married a son of a Spanish conquistador. ²The husband (named Juan de Oñate) wanted to go into an area in the northern part of New Spain, so he crossed the Rio Grande River, and then he traveled north. ³In 1598 he brought the first cattle, sheep, and horses into the area. ⁴This was the first Spanish settlement in present-day New Mexico.

_____ 1. Cortés probably had several granddaughters.

_____ 2. Juan de Oñate was the only son in his family.

_____ 3. We use the article *an* with the word *area* in sentence 2 because we know exact information about this area of New Spain.

_____ 4. We use the article *the* with the word *area* in sentence 3 because this is the same area mentioned in sentence 2.

_____ 5. We use the article *the* with *Rio Grande River* because it is a specific name.

Activity 5

Circle the correct article in parentheses.

Spain colonized (the / a / an) large area north of Mexico City, and different
                                1

kinds of people came to (the / a / an) area. During (the / a / an) Spanish
                                  2   3

colonial period, there was (the / a / an) blending of people between
                                    4

(the / a / an) Spaniards and (the / a / an) Native Americans. (The / A / An)
         5   6   7

blending of these people produced (the / a / an) interesting new culture.
                                                8

Many modern Mexicans and Mexican Americans descended from

(the / a / an) blended new culture.
         9

Activity 6

A. *Fill in each blank space with* a, an, *or* the.

_____ traditions of _____ Spanish people blended with
          1   2

_____ traditions of _____ Native Americans. This caused
          3   4

_____ exchange of different traditions within these cultures. For
          5

example, _____ food of _____ people in colonial New
                     6   7

Spain, such as corn, tomatoes, potatoes, and chili peppers became popular

in Spain and other countries in Europe. _____ example of one new
                                                         8

kind of food from _____ New World was something called *tamale*.
                            9

This is _____ mixture of ground beef and chili peppers wrapped in
                 10

corn meal and steamed in corn husks. In addition, _____ new kind
                                                                11

of cooking developed in _____ colony of New Spain because
                                  12

_____ Spanish livestock and sheep brought milk and cheese to
          13

_____ area.
          14

B. *Label each picture* a *or* b *for the sentence that fits.*

1. a. Take the pepper for the tamale.

    b. Take a pepper for the tamale.   _____

2. a. Take the pepper for the tamale.

    b. Take a pepper for the tamale.   _____

3. a. Use an ear of corn for that recipe.

   b. Use the ear of corn for that recipe. ____

4. a. Use an ear of corn for that recipe.

   b. Use the ear of corn for that recipe. ____

Now circle the letter of the sentence (a or b) that fits the picture.

5. a. Steam the tamale in a pot.

   b. Steam the tamale in the pot.

6. a. Jorge wants to eat a tamale.

   b. Jorge wants to eat the tamale.

Activity 7

Find twelve mistakes with incorrect or missing articles and show how to correct them.

1. In an typical area of New Spain, you could find all of the following: a mission (religious building or church), a military post (presidio), town (pueblo), and a ranch (rancho).

2. Some religious men (called friars) settled an large part of area now in California.

3. They converted a local inhabitants to their religion.

4. They made the local Native Americans build missions in many places, such as the Texas and a coast of California.

5. They built an mission in San Diego. It was first mission in California. Each time they built a mission, town started as well. Today a cities of San Antonio, San Diego, Los Angeles, and San Francisco sit on an original Spanish settlements.

Articles

The and Zero Article

¹In the Spanish areas of North America, there were large **ranchos** or haciendas. ²**Cowboys** (called vaqueros) raised livestock on these ranchos. ³Vaqueros developed ranching **techniques** and equipment. ⁴Many parts of cowboy life in the United States come from these vaqueros.

Presentation

Questions

1. Look at the bold words in these sentences. Are these count or non-count nouns? Are they singular or plural? Does an article come before these nouns?

2. Look at the following words in sentences 2, 3, and 4:

     livestock (sentence 2)

     equipment (sentence 3)

     life (sentence 4)

   Are these words count or non-count nouns? Does an article come before each of them?

Explanation—Definite Article *The* and Zero Article

1. In Lesson 17 you learned about using the indefinite (general or not specific) articles *a/an* and the definite article *the* with nouns.

   We use *a/an* only for a single indefinite countable noun.

     A vaquero was *a* cowboy.   *A* vaquero worked on *a* ranch.

   We use *the* for specific nouns. These can be countable (singular or plural) and noncount.

     In *the* Spanish areas of North America, there were many ranchos.

     The livestock on these ranchos included cattle.

2. We cannot use *a/an* for a plural indefinite countable noun. In this case we use no article or what we call *zero article*.

     Vaqueros were *cowboys*.   *Vaqueros* worked on *ranchos*.

3. We also use no article (zero article) for an indefinite (not specific) non-count noun.

> Vaqueros raised *livestock* on these ranchos.

> Vaqueros developed ranching *equipment*.

4. Below is a review of articles. This chart includes information from Lessons 17 and 18.

Indefinite (general/not a specific noun)		Definite (specific noun/something known)
a / an	zero article	*the*
singular count nouns *A* vaquero was *a* cowboy. *A* treaty is *an* agreement.		singular count nouns *The* Conquistador Hernán Cortés conquered Mexico in *the* 16th century.
	plural count nouns *Vaqueros* worked on *ranchos.*	plural count nouns *The* Spanish areas of California had many ranchos.
	non-count nouns Vaqueros developed ranching *equipment.*	non-count nouns *The* food of different people blended in New Spain.

Practice

Activity 1   (Review coordinating conjunctions in *Destinations 1 Writing for Academic Success*—Unit 3, pp. 66–75.)

A. *Above each of the underlined words, put a label as follows:*

- If it is a singular count noun, write SC.
- If it is a plural count noun, write PC.
- If it is a non-count noun, write NC. Follow the examples.

A <u>Vaquero</u> [SC] was usually a *mestizo* or an <u>Indian</u>. <u>Vaqueros</u> [PC] rode <u>horses</u>, and they took care of <u>livestock</u> [NC]. They wore high-heeled <u>boots</u> and large <u>hats</u> for protection against the <u>weather</u>. A <u>vaquero</u> followed <u>animals</u> on open <u>land</u>. These men became lonely, so they often played <u>music</u> on a <u>guitar</u> and sang <u>songs</u>. They also used special <u>vocabulary</u> during their <u>work</u>, and some of these words came into the English <u>language</u>. Some of the <u>words</u> stayed almost the same, but others changed. For example, *rancho* became ranch, and *vaquero* changed into the English <u>word</u> buckaroo.

B. *Circle all the articles in the paragraph above. If there is no article with the underlined noun, write 0 above it.*

Activity 2

A. *On line A write* a, an, *or* 0 *(for no article) in each space of the following sentences.*

B. *On line B rewrite the sentence by changing the underlined count nouns from singular to plural. Follow the example.*

A. _A_ <u>Conquistador</u> came to the New World and took _0_ territory for Spain.

B. _<u>Conquistadors came to the New World and took territory for Spain.</u>_

1. A. _____ <u>Vaquero</u> worked on _____ <u>rancho</u> by taking care of _____ livestock.

   B. _____

2. A. _____ agricultural <u>worker</u> came to _____ <u>farm</u> in California to pick _____ fruit in _____ <u>field</u>.

   B. _____

3. A. _____ <u>immigrant</u> came north to work in _____ <u>mine</u> or to find _____ gold.

   B. _____

4. A. _____ <u>settler</u> came to the United States and found _____ work on _____ <u>railroad</u>.

   B. _____

Activity 3

Circle the correct article or zero article in parentheses.

(The / A / 0) Mexico became (the / an / 0) independent country in 1821.
      1   2

(The / A / 0) new government of (the / 0 / a) Mexico made (a / the / 0)
      3   4   5

changes in several ways. (A / An / 0) important change was to divide
                              6

(the / a / an) valuable mission land among some inhabitants of (a / 0 / the)
      7   8

area. Therefore, much of (0 / the / a) land became large (a / the / 0)
                              9   10

ranchos. Some of this land became (0 / a / an) grazing areas for (a / an / 0)
                                        11   12

livestock. In (the / 0 / a) New Mexico (a / 0 / the) land was perfect for
                  13   14

raising (0 / the / a) sheep. In (the / a / 0) Texas and (0 / a / the) California
                15   16   17
many people became (the / 0 / a) cattle ranchers.
                18

Activity 4   (Review coordinating conjunctions in *Destinations 1 Writing for Academic
                 Success*—Unit 3, pp. 66–75.)

A. *Fill in the spaces with* a, an, the, *or* 0 *(for no article necessary).*

1. In 1848 at the end of _____ Mexican American War, _____ United States
    and _____ Mexico signed _____ treaty.

2. This treaty, _____ Treaty of Guadelupe Hidalgo, ended this war, and it
    gave some Mexican territory to _____ United States.

3. _____ territory was _____ northern half of Mexico's land.

4. _____ treaty also gave _____ Mexican residents (called Californios) living
    in _____ area _____ choice.

5. _____ Californios could stay in _____ territory and become _____ citizens
    of _____ United States, or they could go back to Mexico.

B. *Number the sentences below to put them in good order for a story.*
    (Hint: Use the years in the sentences to help you with the order.)
    Then fill in the spaces with a, an, the, *or* 0 *(for no article necessary).*
    The first one has been done for you.

_____   a. _____ new law hurt _____ Californios, so after 1851 many of
            them lost their land.

_____   b. In 1849 _____ people came to California from other parts of the
            United States to look for _____ gold, and by 1852 _____
            population of California was about 260,000 people.

_____   c. Others went through _____ long or expensive legal battles to
            keep their land.

_____   d. California became _____ U.S. state on September 8, 1850.

__1__   e. In 1848 many of _the_ 15,000 Californios became _the_ first
            Mexican American citizens of _the_ United States through
            the treaty of Guadeloupe Hidalgo.

_____   f. In 1851 _____ United States made _____ new law about land
            ownership.

Activity 5

Each of the following sentences has some words in bold. Look at these bold areas and decide if the use of articles (a/an/the/0 article) is correct.

A. *One sentence is correct and does not need any changes. Put a C next to the number of this sentence.*

B. *All of the other sentences have two mistakes with articles. Find these mistakes and correct them. Look for the following kinds of mistakes in these sentences:*

- incorrect article
- missing article
- extra article (no article is necessary)

1. a. After **a Mexican American War,** both **the economy and population** of **southwest** underwent changes and grew rapidly.

   b. **A new mines** began to open throughout **area.**

   c. The discovery of **a silver, copper, and zinc** in **Arizona** and **Colorado** brought **the miners and settlers** to those areas.

2. a. **Mexican workers** began to work on **railroads** to build **new train lines,** especially through parts of **deserts** in the area.

   b. **A workers** also worked on **the railroads** by repairing and maintaining **a rail lines.**

3. a. **The farmers** encouraged **Mexican hand laborers** to migrate from **the Mexico.**

   b. **The farm workers** picked **a cotton, fruit,** and **vegetables,** but they received **a low wages.**

   c. **Cotton growers** in **Texas** were **first agricultural employers** of **an Mexican labor.**

Activity 6

In this lesson and in Unit Three of Destinations 1 Writing for Academic Success, *you learned about different kinds of people and workers. You will find some of these in List A below. You will also find other nouns from this unit in List B.*

Choose one noun from List A and write 2-3 sentences about that group of people. Use as many of the words in List B as possible in your sentences. Be sure to use correct articles or no article with these nouns. Follow the example.

| **A:** | immigrants | settlers | Vaqueros | miners |
| | agricultural workers | | manual laborers | |

B:	new country	land	jobs	area	southwest
	United States	workers	California	Mexico	horses
	cattle	animals	vegetables	railroads	gold
	silver	fruit	fields	mines	
	ranchos/farms	work			

EXAMPLE: railroad workers

Mexican workers came north to work on railroads in the southwestern area of the United States. Railroad work was difficult. A railroad worker often received low wages. Many workers lived in poor housing near the railroads.

Pronouns

Subject, Object, and Reflexive Pronouns

[1]Many Mexican American immigrants worked in agriculture, but **they** were not all poor farmers. [2]Some of **them** were members of the upper classes. [3]They came here to build new lives, and they helped **themselves** through more business and educational opportunities. [4]Life in the U.S. helped **them** in these areas.

Presentation

Questions

1. Look at the bold word in sentence 1. What other sentence do you find this word in? What does this word refer to in both of those sentences?

2. Look at the bold word in sentence 2. What word does it follow in this sentence? What other sentence do you find this word in? What word does it follow in that sentence?

3. Look at the bold word in sentence 3. What does this word mean?

Explanation—Pronouns

1. We use pronouns to take the place of nouns. When we use a pronoun, we usually want readers or listeners to think of something or someone they know about already. We say a pronoun *refers* to this other noun.

   Many Mexican American immigrants worked in agriculture, but *they* were not all poor farmers.

   In the first clause, the subject is *Mexican American immigrants*. In the second clause, we want to talk about these same people, but we do not want to repeat the exact same words. Therefore, we use the pronoun *they*. In this sentence *they* refers to *Mexican American immigrants*.

2. There are several different kinds of pronouns in English. In this lesson we will discuss and practice three groups: *subject, object,* and *reflexive pronouns.*

   a. You will find *subject* pronouns in the subject position of a sentence. These pronouns include the following:

	singular	plural
First Person	I	we
Second Person	you	you
Third Person	she/he/it	they

   NOTE: We always use a capital letter for the pronoun *I*.

   I came to the United States for my education.
   S V

   My friend came here for a better job, and *he* works at a computer company.
      S   V   S   V

   b. You will find *object* pronouns in the object position of a sentence. These pronouns include the following:

	singular	plural
First Person	me	us
Second Person	you	you
Third Person	her/him/it	them

   Life in the United States could help *them* with a better education or job.
    S   V   O

   That book helped *us* understand more about Mexican American history.
       S   V   O

   You will also find object pronouns after a preposition.

   NOTE: See Unit Two, Lessons 15 and 16 for more information about prepositions.

   Some *of them* were members of the upper class.

   Sometimes an immigrant brought family *with him* to the new country.

   c. *Reflexive* pronouns refer back to the subject of the sentence. These pronouns include the following:

	singular	plural
First Person	myself	ourselves
Second Person	yourself	yourselves
Third Person	himself/herself/itself	themselves

   A vaquero took care of *himself* and his animals.

   Immigrants helped *themselves* through more business and educational opportunities.

NOTE: In the above examples, it is incorrect to say: A vaquero took care of *him* or They helped *them* through more business and educational opportunities because *him* or *them* refers to other people, not the vaquero or immigrants in the subject of the sentence.

Verbs and phrases we commonly use with reflexive pronouns:

ask	cut	help	kill	see	teach
be proud of	enjoy	hurt	look at	take care of	tell
believe in	feel sorry for	introduce	remind	talk to	work for

3. Sometimes we use the pronoun *I* with another word, such as a noun or another pronoun. In this case you should put the pronoun *I* second in order to be more polite.

    José and I enjoy reading about history.

    He and I enjoy reading about history.

4. **Usage Notes**

    a. In conversation native speakers often use the wrong pronoun. You should not write these mistakes. For example, you may hear sentences like the following:

    <u>Me and my brother</u> read the same history book.

    Alicia gave the book <u>to my brother and I</u>.

    What is the correct form for each of the incorrect pronouns in the sentences above?

    b. In the past it was common to use the pronoun *he* to refer to people (and animals sometimes) if the writer or speaker was not sure about the sex. More recently, many people feel writers should not use *he* so often. This is because it seems we are excluding (leaving out) females if you do this.

    Do several things to avoid this situation:

    *   Repeat the noun (and not use a pronoun).
    *   Change your subject to a plural one. This way you will use the pronoun "they." (For example, change "person" to "people.")
    *   Use *he* and *she* together as follows:

        he and she   he or she   s/he   (s)he

    You need to be careful with all of the above suggestions. It can become awkward to use one way too many times.

Practice

Activity 1   (Review coordinating conjunctions in *Destinations 1 Writing for Academic Success*—Unit 3, pp. 66–75.)

   Label each pronoun in bold as follows: S for subject pronoun, O for object pronoun, R for reflexive pronoun. Then draw an arrow from the pronoun to the nouns it refers to. Follow the examples.

EXAMPLES:

In the 1890s many Mexicans came to the United States, but more of **them** left Mexico after 1900.

At that time immigrants did not need passports, so **they** crossed the border easily from Mexico.

1. In 1910 a civil war began in Mexico, and **it** caused thousands of people to come north to the United States.

2. Some people came with their families, so **they** came in groups.

3. Some men came to look for work by **themselves**.

4. A new Mexican immigrant often worked as a laborer. **He** could find work in agriculture, or **he** could find work on a railroad.

5. **I** come from a family of immigrants. **We** arrived in this country over 30 years ago, and my grandparents gave **us** a good start in this country.

6. My grandmother came here with her husband, and **she** worked in the fields with **him**.

7. My uncle arrived in the United States with some money from Mexico. **He** used **it** to buy a small business, so **he** worked for **himself** for many years.

Activity 2 (Review coordinating conjunctions in *Destinations 1 Writing for Academic Success*—Unit 3, pp. 66–75.)

Circle the correct word in parentheses in the following sentences.

A. In the 1800s many Chinese immigrants came to the United States, and

many of (they / them) worked on the railroads. In 1882 U.S. lawmakers
         1

passed a law, and (it / they) called (them / it) the Chinese Exclusion Act.
                       2   3

(It / He) stopped Chinese immigration into the U.S. and created a need
   4

for new railroad workers. Mexican laborers continued to come into the

country, so it became easier for (them / they) to find work on the
                                 5

railroads. (They / Them) built new tracks and repaired existing lines.
            6

B. In 1885 some friends and (me / I) came up from Mexico, but (us / we)
                             1   2

had trouble finding jobs. Finally, a railroad company hired one friend

and (I / me) to work on a new railroad. On this job (we / us) put up
     3   4

new rail lines through parts of the desert. Many of (we / us) needed to
                                                     5

live near our work. (Me / I) lived in a boxcar by (myself / ourselves),
                     6   7

and my friend lived in another one next to (I / me).
                                            8

Activity 3

Fill in each space in the following sentences with a reflexive pronoun. Do not use any other kind of pronoun in these spaces. The first one has been done as an example.

1. Workers often joined community organizations to help

   _____*themselves*_____.

2. I went to a meeting and introduced _____.

3. Another worker also came to the meeting, and she introduced

   _____.

4. Both she and I enjoyed _____ at the meeting.

5. Many workers came to this country alone, so they had to take care of

    _____.

6. Sometimes a worker hurt _____ on the job and

    needed some outside help.

7. If you succeed on a job, you should be proud of _____.

Activity 4

Fill in the spaces with the correct pronoun from the list given.

they	it	themselves

A. Mexican workers on the railroads and in the mines often came to the

    United States by _____. _____ earned
                        1   2

    money and sent _____ back home to their families.
                        3

it	he	they	himself

B. In the early 20th century Mexican Americans mined silver in the

    Southwest. On this job _____ had to work very hard
                                1

    taking out the silver from inside the mines. Each miner filled a sack with

    silver ore and carried _____ by _____ to the
                                2   3

    surface from the mine. _____ had to be strong to do this
                                4

    because each sack weighed about 200 pounds.

us	ourselves	we	I

C. One worker said: My family and _____ worked together
                                        1

    in the fields. _____ all contributed to the work, from
                        2

    the very young to the very old. All of _____ contributed
                                              3

    to the family's income this way. We always tried to take care of

    _____.
        4

(Review coordinating conjunctions in *Destinations 1 Writing for Academic Success*—Unit 3, pp. 66–75.)

Use any pronoun for each space. Some spaces may have more than one possible answer.

D. Migrant workers moved from farm to farm and state to state looking for work. One young worker described his work as follows: In the summer

_____ help my father every day in the strawberry fields.
1

_____ are large fields, and _____ work hard
2   3

to pick the strawberries. Sometimes my father and _____
4

stop to eat. _____ eat strawberries, or _____
5   6

brings beans for _____ to have for lunch. Most of the
7

workers rest at lunch for a short time, and then _____ all
8

go back to work.

Activity 5 (Review coordinating conjunctions in *Destinations 1 Writing for Academic Success*—Unit 3, pp. 66–75.)

Below a woman describes her work in the cotton fields of Texas in the 1920s. Each sentence has one or two mistakes with pronouns. Find the mistakes and correct them.

1. My family went to the field early in the morning, so all of we were there by 5 a.m.

2. My family and me wanted to start work right away, but the owner didn't let him.

3. My father often brought many people in a truck to work with we.

4. He was responsible for they and received some extra money for bringing him.

5. Sometimes my father helped I with my work.

6. I enjoyed working with he, but often I had to work by himself.

7. At noon most workers stopped work, so them could eat lunch for about 15 minutes.

8. After lunch the work became slow because the cotton was dry, and they was more difficult to put in the bags.

9. At the end of the day the owners gave wages to ourselves.

10. Them paid us according to how much the cotton weighed.

Possessives

Possessive Nouns

[1]Spaniards introduced sheep to **New Mexico's** economy, and raising sheep remained important in that area. [2]My **friend's** family owned a sheep farm there for many years. [3]A **sheepherder's** life was often difficult and lonely.

Presentation

Questions

1. Look at the words in bold in these sentences. What information does the *'s* give? (Why is the *'s* at the end of these words?)

2. What kind of word follows each of the bold words with the *'s*?

3. Look at the word *Spaniards* in sentence 1 (the first word in the sentence) and the word *years* in sentence 2 (the last word in the sentence). Why don't these words have an apostrophe (*'*) before the *-s*?

Explanation—Possessive Nouns

1. A possessive noun shows ownership. It tells you who or what something belongs to. We show possession with nouns as follows:

    a. Use *'s* at the end of a singular noun.

    EXAMPLES: a friend's family   a sheepherder's life   a worker's wages

    NOTE: These examples have the same meaning as *a family of a friend* or *a life of a sheepherder*.

    b. Add only an apostrophe (*'*) at the end of a plural noun that ends in *-s*.

    EXAMPLES: the sheepherders' work   the workers' wages
    (more than one sheepherder)   (more than one worker)

c. If a singular noun or name already ends in an -s, we use either the apostrophe -s ('s) ending or just the apostrophe after the -s'. This may depend on how awkward the pronunciation of the word is with the 's.

EXAMPLES: the boss's /the boss' rules   Luis'/Luis's sheep farm

d. Be careful with irregular noun plurals such as women, children, and men. These forms do not have the plural -s ending because they are irregular. Therefore, they follow the regular rule about adding the 's.

men's wages   women's jobs   children's schools

2. A possessive will usually have at least two words, such as *José's farm* or *Marta's uncle*.

Sometimes you will find only one word in a possessive, especially after a noun has already been mentioned. Then the speaker or writer may not repeat the noun.

Is that *José's farm?*   No it's *Marta's*.

(It is not necessary to repeat the word *farm* in the second sentence.)

3. If two people own the same thing, only the second person adds the apostrophe -s.

EXAMPLE: He is working on *José and Marta's farm*.

4. You will often find possessives with names of people, places, or companies (proper nouns).

EXAMPLES: New Mexico's economy   José's uncle

We also usually use possessive nouns for other living things (such as animals) and a few non-living things such as time and nature.

EXAMPLES: Workers in the fields need protection from the *sun's rays*.

The *livestock's water supply* was getting low.

We do not usually use the possessive nouns for other non-living things (such as things or ideas). For these, we use the preposition *"of."*

EXAMPLES: I love *the color of that house*.

The hours of that job are long and difficult.

Practice

Activity 1   (Review coordinating conjunctions in *Destinations 1 Writing for Academic Success*—Unit 3, pp. 66–75.)

Circle each possessive noun. Then put a line under each plural noun.

1. Mexican American immigrants often lived near their jobs.

2. A farm worker's housing was usually near the fields. Sometimes these workers lived in a grower's buildings. These buildings could be small, so a family's home was often a shack of one or two rooms for parents, children, and perhaps grandparents or other relatives.

3. A railroad worker's home was often a boxcar. Sometimes workers lived in a group of these cars near the train lines, and these people's homes often formed communities or *colonias*.

4. Miners usually lived in settlements as well. The miners' homes could be rough adobe huts near the mines.

Activity 2   (Review coordinating conjunctions in *Destinations 1 Writing for Academic Success*—Unit 3, pp. 66–75.)

Fill in each space with the possessive form of the word given in parentheses. Follow the example.

EXAMPLE: (company) During World War I, many U.S. men became soldiers, so Mexican workers often filled a _____company's_____ need for workers.

1. (women)   Mexican _____ jobs were often in manufacturing, such as garment factories.

2. (economy)   The _____ success in the 1920s was helpful to Mexican American immigrants, so many of them found jobs.

3. (people)   There was a growing demand for _____ unskilled labor.

4. (government)   The _____ immigration laws limited the number of Asians and Eastern Europeans entering the United States, but these laws did not affect Mexican immigration.

5. (immigrants)   The Mexican _____ visas made them legal residents of the U.S.

6. (newcomers)   At first, _____ jobs were often in agriculture or mining, but later they found employment opportunities in other areas.

7. (industries)   The meatpacking and manufacturing _____ jobs became more available in the 1920s, so many Mexican Americans worked in those industries.

Activity 3

A. *Fill in the spaces with the words in parentheses using the possessive form. Be sure to put the words in correct order. Follow the example.*

EXAMPLE:

The U.S. Government issued ___contract workers' documents___ to
                              (documents/contract workers)
Mexicans during World War II.

1. Two _____ (the U.S. and Mexico) agreed on
        (countries/governments)
establishing the Bracero Program in 1942.

2. This _____ during the war created a need
        (labor shortage/country)
for these workers.

3. The _____ allowed them to stay in the
       (Braceros/work permits)
United States for a limited time.

4. A _____ were often difficult and dangerous,
     (working conditions /Bracero)
but many Mexican men wanted to work in the program.

5. The largest number of workers came during the _____.
    (third phase/program)

6. These _____ to the war effort included
    (men/contributions)

    transporting soldiers and supplies on the railroads.

B. *Fill in the spaces with the two words in parentheses using the possessive
    form. Be sure to put the words in correct order. If the words should not be
    possessive, use the* noun + of *pattern. Follow the examples.*

    EXAMPLES:

    The _____worker's name_____ is Jorge, and he works in
            (worker/name)

    a meat-packing plant.

    The _____hours of the job_____ are long each day.
            (job/hours)

1. After the treaty of Guadalupe Hidalgo, many _____
    (Mexican Americans/lives)

    changed.

2. A _____ in the southwestern part of the U.S.
      (blending/cultures)

    took place during Spanish rule.

3. The _____ depended on ranching for a while.
       (southwest/economy)

4. Migrant workers often find seasonal work, so their _____
    (lives/families)

    depend on different kinds of jobs in different places.

5. Many jobs in the southwest depend on the _____,
    (resources/earth)

    such as farmland and silver or copper ore deposits.

6. The _____ in the cotton field is often gray.
       (equipment/color)

7. _____ include stories of people from many
    (California and Texas/histories)

    different backgrounds.

W *Activity 4* (Review coordinating conjunctions in *Destinations 1 Writing for Academic Success*—Unit 3, pp. 66–75.)

A. *Add an apostrophe to show possession to five of the bold nouns in the paragraph below. Two of these bold nouns do not need the apostrophe.*

My aunt Luisa lived on her **grandparents** sheep farm, and she remembers many of the **workers** there. Luisa especially remembers one of her **grandmothers sheepherders.** He was an old man, and Luisa often went with her grandmother to visit this **mans** sheep camp. **Luisas** thoughts about this place were sad and depressing, but the old man always seemed happy. She remembers this **workers** whistling and singing in the distance during her visits.

B. *Add an apostrophe to show possession to five nouns in the following sentences. (Do not add any letters or other punctuation.)*

During the 1920s the United States economy grew, so business demand for unskilled labor was high. Between 1920 and 1929 approximately 600,000 Mexican workers came to the United States with visas. These workers visas gave them legal residence but not citizenship in this country. The United States established a police for the border, and this Border Patrols job was to control undocumented workers entrance into the U.S.

Activity 5

A. *Find three mistakes with apostrophes and show how to correct them.*
   (Not all of the apostrophes on possessive nouns are incorrect.)

From the 1870s into the 20th century, Mexican American's established
many different helpful organizations. Some of the Mexican communitys'
organizations, called *Mutualistas,* helped people adapt to living in a new
country. A mutualistas work included publishing Spanish-language
newspapers, building schools, and helping people with healthcare. One
organization's membership included thousands of people from all over the
Southwest.

B. *Some of the possessive nouns in the following sentences are correct, and*
   some are not. Correct the ones that are wrong. If a sentence is correct,
   write C next to the number.

1. An immigrants journey to a new country can be long and difficult.

2. Some people know much about their ancestors' stories.

3. Henry Cisneros' knowledge of his familys' origins is extensive.

4. Henrys' family descends from Spaniards and mestizos.

Possessives

Possessive Adjectives and Pronouns

[1]This is a photo of Juan Garcia's family. [2]**His grandparents** came to the U.S. from Mexico. [3]**Their children** were born in the United States. [4]Juan and his wife both grew up in California. [5]The youngest children in this photograph are **theirs.**

Presentation

Questions

1. Circle the possessive noun in sentence 1.

2. Look at the possessives in bold in sentences 2 and 3. How are the possessives in these two sentences different from the possessive noun in sentence 1?

3. Look at the bold word at the end of sentence 5. How is this a different kind of possessive than the one at the beginning of sentence 3?

Explanation—Possessive Adjectives and Pronouns

1. The following chart shows two groups of possessive words in English. Notice that we do not put an apostrophe on any of the words on this chart.

Possessive Adjectives	Possessive Pronouns
my	mine
your	yours
his	his
her	hers
its	—
our	ours
their	theirs

2. Possessive adjectives and pronouns show that something belongs to
    someone (ownership or possession).

    a. The photo belongs to my mother.   b. It is *her* photo.   c. It is *hers*.
    possessive adjective   possessive pronoun

    NOTE: Sentences *b* and *c* have the same meaning.

3. We use possessive adjectives before a noun and possessive pronouns
    without a noun.

    This is *Juan Garcia's* family. *His grandparents* came to the U.S. from Mexico.
    possessive noun   possessive adjective + noun

    Juan and Maria have two children. The youngest in the photograph
    are *theirs*.
    possessive pronoun

    Speakers often use a possessive pronoun when they do not want to repeat
    the noun of possession. You will usually find these possessives more in
    speaking than in writing.

4. Be especially careful about using the word *its* as a possessive (without an
    apostrophe) and *it's*, the contraction of *it is* or *it has*. You should only use
    the apostrophe if you can change the word to *it is* or *it has* in the sentence.

    I enjoy learning about my family history. *It's (it is)* a fascinating subject.

    It's (it has*) been an interesting subject to study.

    I want to learn more about my family and *its history.*

5. Sometimes we use a possessive adjective and a possessive noun together.

    My friend's family comes from Mexico.

    Her father's parents were farmers there.

---

*You will learn more about using this verb form *(has + verb)* in Unit Six.

Practice

Activity 1

Use the family tree below to complete both parts of this activity.

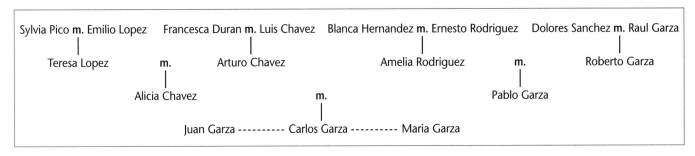

Sylvia Pico **m.** Emilio Lopez   Francesca Duran **m.** Luis Chavez   Blanca Hernandez **m.** Ernesto Rodriguez   Dolores Sanchez **m.** Raul Garza

Teresa Lopez   **m.**   Arturo Chavez   Amelia Rodriguez   **m.**   Roberto Garza

Alicia Chavez   **m.**   Pablo Garza

Juan Garza ---------- Carlos Garza ---------- Maria Garza

A. *The following is a short description of part of Carlos Garza's family. Circle each possessive adjective and underline each possessive noun in the paragraph.*

Pablo is his father, and Roberto is one of his grandfathers. His mother Alicia's grandparents on her father's side are Francesca Duran and Luis Chavez. Her parents are Teresa Lopez and Arturo Chavez. Carlos is their grandson.

B. *Now imagine you are Blanca Hernandez on this family tree. Fill in the blank spaces about your family with one of the family words from the list below. Use a different word for each answer.*

| sister | wife | husband | daughter | grandson | son-in-law | son |

Ernesto Rodriguez is my _____, and we have three great
grandchildren: Juan, Carlos, and Maria Garza. Our _____ is
Amelia. She married Roberto Garza, so he is our _____. My
_____ is Pablo Garza, and his _____ is Alicia
Chavez. Their _____ is Carlos, and his _____
is Maria.

Activity 2

Maria, Carlos Garza's sister, decided to learn more about their family and their ancestors. Below you will find some information about how she began to do this. Choose the correct word in parentheses for each sentence.

Maria found two local genealogy clubs and went to a few of

(theirs / theirs' / their) meetings. She joined one club because it gave
     1

a lot of help to (it's / its / its') new members. She became friends with one
            2

of the members and attended (his'/ his / his's) workshop for beginners.
             3

He explained step-by-step how to begin a family search, and Maria became

anxious to start (her / her's / hers).
          4

    After the workshop she called (hers / her's / her) parents and asked
               5

them to write down the names of all of (their / theirs / theirs') relatives.
               6

Then she asked (her / her's / hers) mother to contact some of
         7

(her / hers / her's) family and (her's / hers / her) father to contact
   8   9

some of (his / his' / his's) for more information.
      10

Activity 3   (Review coordinating conjunctions in *Destinations 1 Writing for Academic Success*—Unit 3, pp. 66–75.)

A.   *Maria continued her family research, and Carlos asked her about it. Fill the blank spaces in Maria's explanation with one of the possessive adjectives or pronouns below. Use a different word for each answer.*

hers	theirs	his	her	our	their	my

I talked to several relatives and asked them to share _____ stories.
                                                      1

First, I talked to _____ parents and grandparents. Mom told me
                    2

stories about _____ grandparents, and I even asked Aunt Irma and
                  3

Uncle Jorge to tell me _____ . Uncle Jorge remembered several
                    4

stories about _____ family, but Aunt Irma couldn't remember too
                  5

much about _____ . I still need to speak with several more people,
               6

so I'll continue _____ research as much as possible.
                 7

B. *Maria's friend wants to learn about her family history, so she asked Maria for some information and suggestions about this. Fill in the blank spaces in Maria's answer with the following pronouns. You will need to use some of these words more than once. In these cases the number of times is in parentheses next to the word.*

| my | your (3) | its | his | her (3) | our | their (3) | yours | hers |

To learn about _____ family history, you need to talk to as many
                        1

family members as possible. Talk to parents, grandparents, aunts, and

uncles about _____ lives and experiences. Sometimes it's not easy
                    2

to get family information, but each family has _____ story, so
                                                    3

don't give up.

Here's how you can start:

- Ask each relative to take the time to talk to you about _____ or
                                                              4

  _____ life story.
        5

- Ask all your relatives to find _____ old photos and papers. Then
                                        6

  they can tell stories about these. You can also share _____
                                                              7

  with them.

- Help _____ relatives remember _____ stories
            8   9

  by asking them questions. For example, you could say, "Do you

  remember about a favorite time with _____ grandparents?
                                            10

  I remember we took a trip to San Francisco with them, but I was too

  young to remember much about it."

- Make a recording of _____ talks with relatives. Begin each one
                            11

  with an introduction. For example, you might say, "This is Maria Garza.

  I'm interviewing _____ grandmother, Teresa Lopez, on
                        12

  June 2, 2007. This is _____ 65th birthday, and we are talking
                              13

  about _____ life and family in general. I am asking her about
              14

  the lives of several people in the family, but I am especially interested

  in _____."
          15

Activity 4   (Review coordinating conjunctions in *Destinations 1 Writing for Academic Success*—Unit 3, pp. 66–75.)

Maria contacted several relatives, and some of them sent responses. Below you will find some of the responses, but each one has two or three problems with possessives. Find the mistakes and correct them.

1. Maria's grandparents sent a copy of theirs' marriage certificate. They also sent a few pictures of their wedding's day.

2. Hers aunt sent some information on a family tree. She wrote, "This page has part of ours family tree on it. It's not complete, but maybe you can compare it with your's. I hope this helps."

3. An uncle sent him a copy of her birth certificate with this note: "Here's a copy of mine birth certificate. I thought I had a copy of my too, but now I can't find it. I'll keep looking for it."

4. Maria's other relatives did not answer him. She will wait for a few more, or she will try to look up theirs information by herself.

Activity 5

A. *Draw your own family tree. Then write five sentences about people in your family using possessive nouns and any of the possessive adjectives and pronouns from this lesson.*

    You may write about one person and write all your sentences about that person, or you may write about different people.

    EXAMPLES: My mother's name is Evelyn. Her family lives in Toronto.

    Our family visits my grandparents often.

    _____

    _____

    _____

    _____

B. *Discuss your family tree with a partner. Tell your partner some information about some of the people in your family using possessive nouns, adjectives, and pronouns.*

    Write sentences about the information you learned about your partner's family.

    _____

    _____

    _____

    _____

    _____

INTRODUCTION TO MODAL AUXILIARIES

As you saw in Unit One, sometimes verbs work by themselves and sometimes they work with a helping verb or *auxiliary*.

EXAMPLES: 1. She usually *leaves* for work at 7:00 a.m.
  verb

2. Today she *is leaving* later for work.
  auxiliary + verb

One group of auxiliaries has a special name. These words are called *modals*. The nine modals in English are:

can   could   may   might   should   must   will   would   shall

1. These words all have different meanings, and we use them in different situations. In Unit Four you will learn about and practice most of these modals.

    NOTE: This book will not discuss the use of *shall*.

2. We use a modal before a verb. All nine of the modals follow some rules of grammar that do not change.

    RULE 1: Do not add an ending to a modal. In other words, do not add *-s*, *-ed*, or *-ing*.

    Correct: He **can type** quickly on the computer.

    Incorrect: He **cans type** quickly on the computer.

    RULE 2: Do not add an ending to the verb after a modal.

    Correct: She **might ask** her boss for a raise.

    Incorrect: She **might asks** her boss for a raise.

    RULE 3: Do not add the word "to" between a modal and a verb.

    Correct: We **might take** a coffee break at 10:00 a.m.

    Incorrect: We **might to take** a coffee break at 10:00 a.m.

    RULE 4: Do not use more than one modal next to each other.

    Correct: She might ask for a raise today.

    Incorrect: They can **might** ask for a raise today.

3. There are some two and three word expressions that have the same meanings as the modals. However, these expressions do not follow all of the same grammar rules as the modals. Some people call these *equivalent expressions* or *semi-modals*.

Following are some of these expressions that you will learn about in Unit 4.

a. be able to = can/could

b. ought to = should

c. had better = (strong) should

d. have to = must

Ability

Can/Could/Be Able To

[1]Employees at this factory **can work** on a staggered schedule. [2]However, they need to work every day, so they **cannot work** a compressed workweek. [3]In the past some office workers **could have** special four-day work schedules, but the company changed the rules.

Presentation 1

Questions

1. Circle the words in bold that come before the verbs in sentences 1 and 3. What is the meaning of these words?

2. What is the time in sentence 2? What is the time in sentence 3?

Explanation—*Can and Could*

1. Both *can* and *could* express ability in English.

2. *Can* and *could* are both modal auxiliaries (helping verbs). They follow all the grammar rules found in the introduction to modals on pages 146–147.

   Those employees *can work* a staggered schedule.

   In the past some workers *could have* a compressed workweek.

3. **Negative sentences**

   Follow the rule for making a sentence negative.

RULE: Add the word *not* after the auxiliary (helping verb).

Those employees *cannot* (can't**)* work a compressed workweek.

They *could not (couldn't)*** have a staggered schedule last year.

*NOTE: can + not = cannot in writing. It is the only modal that joins with *not* as one word.

****Native speakers often use contractions in conversation. We do not usually use these forms in formal writing.

Follow this pattern for negative sentences using *can* and *could:*

subject	auxiliary (helping verb)	not	verb (simple form)	
Those employees	*can-	not	work	a compressed workweek.
They	could	not	have	a staggered schedule last year.

4. **Questions**

   a. *Yes/No* **questions**

Move the modal (helping verb) to the left of the subject of the sentence. End the sentence with a question mark.

Can those employees *work* a compressed workweek?

Could they *work* a staggered schedule last year?

Follow this pattern for *yes/no* questions using *can* and *could:*

auxiliary (helping verb)	subject	verb (simple form)	
Can	those employees	work	a compressed workweek?
Could	they	work	a staggered schedule last year?

   b. **Question word questions**

Put the question word and the modal to the left of the subject.

How can those workers *change* their schedule?

When could they *work* a compressed workweek?

Follow this pattern for question word questions using *can* and *could:*

question word	auxiliary (helping verb)	subject	verb (simple form)	
How	can	those workers	change	their schedule?
Where	can	they	go	for their break?
When	could	they	work	a compressed workweek?
Who	can	*	work	a compressed workweek?

*NOTE: Do not include a subject in these questions because the answer to *Who* is the subject.

5. We use *could* in different time frames, such as past, present, and future. However, we do not use *can* in the past.

Correct: In the past they *could schedule* a compressed workweek.

In the future they *could schedule* a different kind of workweek.

Incorrect: In the past they *can schedule* a compressed workweek.

In addition, we use *could* for past ability when we are talking about something that was true in general in the past. We do not use it for something that was true for one time only.

Correct: I could work a staggered work schedule last year.

Incorrect: Yesterday I could get a raise at work.

Practice

Activity 1

Circle the modals of ability (can/could) *and the verb that follows them. After each sentence, write the time as past, present, general, or future. The first one has been done as an example.*

1. In a traditional job most employees (can have) a five-day workweek of eight hours a day.   *general*

2. In the past many employers could tell their employees to work longer hours and more than five days a week.

3. Today most workers can arrive to work at 8:00 or 9:00 a.m. and leave by 5:00 p.m.

4. Years ago most workers could not ask for personal or unusual schedules at work.

5. Employees can change their schedules in nontraditional ways at many jobs these days.

6. Most employees could not create nontraditional jobs for themselves in the past.

7. Perhaps in the future more workers could try to work from home or telecommute.

Activity 2   (Review transitions in *Destinations 1 Writing for Academic Success*—Unit 4, pp. 98–105.)

Complete the following sentences by adding can, cannot, could, *or* could not.

1. Today some workers _____ work at home. However, other workers _____ do that.

2. Often new employees _____ have vacation time during their first few months of work.

3. At my old job I _____ have three weeks of vacation. On the other hand, I _____ take all of them at the same time.

4. At my present job I _____ take any amount of vacation time all at once.

5. In the past in this country some children had jobs. As a result, they _____ go to school.

6. Today we have child labor laws in this country. Therefore, children _____ work instead of going to school.

Activity 3

Fill in the blanks with either can *or* could *and one of the verbs given. Make the sentence negative where indicated. Use each verb only one time.*

Verbs:	work	be	stay	earn	drive	take

1. My friend Joe _____ extra money at work through overtime.

2. My boss says that I *(negative)* _____ any overtime hours.

3. Last year at my old job I _____ more flexible and work longer hours for more pay.

4. Tomorrow my car will be in the repair shop, so I *(negative)* _____ to work by myself.

5. However, my friend Joe _____ me home from work then.

6. He _____ late at work to wait for me and earn extra pay.

Presentation 2

Questions

1. Circle the words in bold that come before the verbs in sentences 1 and 2. What is the meaning of these words? Why is the first word different in each of these cases?

2. What is the time in sentence 4? How do you know this?

3. What rule do sentences 3 and 4 follow to make these expressions negative?

¹My friend Jean **is able to** share her job with another worker. ²In this way both of them **are able to** work part time each day. ³Jean **is not able to** work full time, so this situation is perfect for her. ⁴Before this job she **was not able to** work at all because of her schedule problems.

Explanation—*Be Able To*

1. The expression *be able to* also expresses ability, but it does not follow all the same grammar rules as *could* and *can*.

2. The expression *be able to* changes to fit the sentence.

    a. It changes to fit the subject of the sentence.

    My friend is able to share her job with another worker.

    Both of them *are* able to work part time.

    b. It changes to fit the time.

    Now she *is* able to work full time.

    In the past they *were* not able to work at all.

3. Sometimes people use contractions with *be able to*.

    She's able to share a job with her coworker.

    They're able to work part time.

    NOTE: You will **not** find these contractions with *be able to* when it is used for past time.

Activity 4 (Review transitions in *Destinations 1 Writing for Academic Success*—Unit 4, pp. 98–105.)

Circle all the words and expressions that show ability. Then underline the verbs that follow each of those.

1. Bill can work from 6:00 a.m. to 3:00 p.m. every day on his new job. Other workers in his department are able to have different hours, such as 7:00 a.m. to 4:00 p.m. However, the employees in his company cannot arrive later than 9:00 a.m. or leave before 3:00 p.m. In other words, those are the company's core hours.

2. Linda is able to spend most of her time working at home because her job involves telecommuting. Last month her boss said she could start working at home and communicate with the office through email and faxes. In other words, she was able to create her own office at home. Now she can complete her work any time of the day. In addition, she is still able to keep in touch with her office during business hours.

Activity 5

Complete the following sentences about abilities by doing two things:

A. *Choose the verb that fits each blank from the list below. Use each verb only one time.*

have	quit	get	be	make	establish	find

B. *Add a form of* be able to *to each sentence. Be sure to change this expression to fit the subject and time. Make your answer negative if indicated.*

1. Last year Gregg _____ his office job and become a freelance computer software trainer.

2. At his old job he *(negative)* _____ his own schedule.

3. Freelancers _____ more flexibility with their work days and times.

4. Now Gregg _____ his own boss, and he is very happy about that.

5. However, sometimes this job is more difficult for Gregg because sometimes freelance workers *(negative)* _____ new companies to work for.

6. Therefore, Gregg _____ his own hours, but he *(negative)* _____ enough work.

Activity 6

Find nine mistakes in the sentences below and correct them.

1. Bob cans type 50 wpm (words per minute) on the computer, but he no is able to type faster than that without making mistakes.

2. Last year Soraya can take a training class for her job. However, this year she cannot to take any classes because her schedule changed at work.

3. Steven's boss is not able help him today with his new project, but she could helps him tomorrow.

4. Yesterday I am not able to go to work because I was sick. I feel a little better today, so I can am able to go. Of course, I also could to stay home one more day because I have a lot of unused sick leave.

Activity 7

A. *Below you will find requirements for a job at a factory. Put a check (✔) next to each of the items on the list that you have the ability to do. Put an ✗ next to each item on the list you are not able to do.*

_____ lift 40-pound packages

_____ put small pieces together easily

_____ be comfortable doing repetitive work

_____ operate a fork lift

_____ use a computer to enter data

_____ work on weekends or at night

_____ understand spoken instructions in English

_____ understand written instructions in English

_____ stand in the same place for long periods of time

_____ hear and understand warnings on a loud speaker system in English

_____ write clearly in English to fill out forms

_____ answer phones and take messages in English

B. *Write sentences using* can, could, *and* be able to *using five of the items in section A. Write some sentences about what you can do and some about what you cannot do. Write some of your sentences about the things you could do in the past as well.*

EXAMPLES:

In the past I could (I was able to) work nights. Now I cannot

(am not able to) work nights, but I can (am able to) work on weekends.

_____

_____

_____

_____

_____

_____

C. *Now interview a classmate and write some of his/her answers below.*

_____

_____

_____

_____

_____

Requests and Permission

Would/Will/Could/May/Can

Presentation

New employee to stranger: [1]**Would** you please show me the way to Steve Howell's office?
Employee to coworker: [2]**Could** you show me the way to Steve Howell's office?
Two good friends: [3]**Can** you show me the way to Steve Howell's office?

Questions

1. Look at the requests for directions to Steve Howell's office in sentences 1, 2, and 3 above. Is each one exactly the same for each situation? Explain why they are or are not the same.

2. Look at the first word of each request. How are these modals different? Which requests are more formal? Are any of them more informal?

3. Think about how you make the same requests in the same situations in **your native language.** Are these three requests exactly the same in your language? If not, how are they different?

Explanation—Modals for Making Requests/ Asking for Permission

1. When we make a request (ask for something), we often use modals. Some of these modals are:

    would   could   will   can

    a. In requests, some modals are more formal or more polite than others.

    b. If you want to be very direct (and most informal), you can also make a request using an imperative form. (Review Lesson 1, page 1 for more information about imperatives.)

    c. You may also want to add *please* to your requests when you want to be more polite.

    can   will   could   would

    direct ◄————————————————————► polite

    d. Most requests are in the form of a question. This means that we follow question word order. Use the following pattern at the beginning of most requests:

    modal + subject + verb (simple form—no endings)

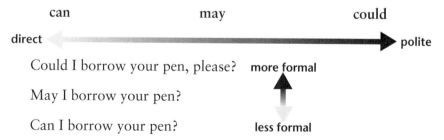

    Would you please show me the way to his office?   **more formal/polite**

    Could you show me the way to his office?

    Will you show me the way to his office, please?

    Can you show me the way to his office?

    Show me the way to his office.   **less formal/more direct**

2. When we want to make a request for permission, we use different modals as well. We often use *could, may,* or *can.*

    can   may   could

    direct ◄————————————————————► polite

    Could I borrow your pen, please?   **more formal**

    May I borrow your pen?

    Can I borrow your pen?   **less formal**

    NOTE: Some people feel that it is not acceptable to use *can* for permission, but native speakers often use it this way.

3. **Answering requests**

    a. Often native speakers give short answers to requests such as:

    •Sure.   • Okay.   • Certainly.   • No Problem.   • Go right ahead.

      b. Often we try to say *No* to a request politely by using the word *sorry* and giving a reason.

         Q: Could you give me a ride home from work?

         A: Sorry, I took the bus today.

      c. We do not use *would* or *could* in answers to requests.

4. **Answering requests for permission**

      a. We use *may* and *can* in answers to permission, but we do not use *could* in these answers.

         Q: Could/May/Can I borrow your pen?

         A: Yes, you may/can.

      b. In negative answers to requests for permission, we use *may not* or *cannot*. We do not use *could not*.

         Q: Could/May/Can I give you the report tomorrow?

         A: No, you may not/cannot.

Sometimes we use the contraction *(can't)* but there is no contraction for *may not*.

Practice

Activity 1

You need some information about how to put together a new desk. You don't have instructions, but the people listed below do have papers with this information. How will you ask each person to see those instructions? Write the letter(s) of your answers in the space provided. More than one answer is possible for each.

a. Would you please show me those instructions?

b. Can you show me your instructions?

c. Will you show me those instructions?

d. Could you show me those instructions?

e. Show me those instructions.

f. Please show me those instructions.

g. May I look at those instructions?

h. Can I see those instructions?

_____ 1. your friend at work

_____ 2. your grandfather

_____ 3. a coworker you don't know

_____ 4. your younger sister

_____ 5. your supervisor at work

_____ 6. your instructor at school

Activity 2

A. It is time for lunch and you are at work. You are hungry, but you have no money to buy lunch. You want to borrow money to buy some food. Look at the list of modals below and choose one for each sentence. Think about how formal or polite you want to be for each one. Be prepared to explain your answers. (Some answers may have more than one possibility.)

can	would	could	may	will

1. (to your best friend at the office) _____ I borrow $5.00 for lunch?

2. (to another worker—you don't know her very well) _____ you lend me some money for lunch today?

3. (to the new employee working next to you) _____ you lend me some money for lunch today?

4. (to your boss) _____ I please borrow some money for lunch?

B. Read the following conversations with requests and responses and fill in each space with one of the choices below. You will not use all of the choices. Some spaces may have more than one possible answer.

can	may	could	cannot	can't	may not	could not

1. Employee: Good morning, Mr. Trent. _____ I talk to you

a
    about my vacation time?

    Boss: I have an important meeting to go to, and I

    _____ talk about that now. You

b

    _____ make an appointment with my

c

    secretary for later in the day.

2. Employee: Good afternoon, Mr. Trent. My family is celebrating my

    mother's 90th birthday next week in Los Angeles.

    _____ I have an extra vacation day in order to

a

    attend the party?

    Boss: I like to try to be flexible with my employees' time off, so I

    want to accommodate you. You _____ take

b

    Friday off if you can find someone to take your shift for you.

3. **Employee:** Hi Jason. I have a favor to ask you. _____ you
   a
   work my shift next Friday? I need to go to Los Angeles for
   the weekend.

   Jason: No, I _____ . I am taking that day off too.
   b
   Sorry.

4. **Employee:** Bill, _____ you take my shift at work next
   Friday, so I can go to Los Angeles with my family?

   Bill: Sure. No problem.

Activity 3

*Choose the most polite and appropriate question and answer for each situation
in the pictures below. Be prepared to explain your answers.*

1.

Question: a. Could you give me some paper for my printer?

b. Give me some paper for my printer.

Answer: a. No. I don't have any for you.

b. Sorry. I don't have any extra paper.

2.

Question: a. Will you open the door now?

b. Would you please open the door for me?

Answer: a. Sure, I can help you with that.

b. I'm busy. I can't help you now.

3.

Question: a. Do you need help?

b. May I help you with something?

Answer: a. No thanks. I can find something by myself.

b. No, I don't.

4.

Question: a. Hello. Could you please give me the Human Resources Department?

b. I want the Human Resources Department.

Answer: a. Hold on. Just a minute.

b. Could you hold a moment, please?

5.

Question: a. Can I have those napkins?

b. Would you please pass those napkins to me?

Answer: a. Sure.

b. In a minute.

6.

Question: a. Can I return this purchase here?

b. Give me my money back for this, please.

Answer: a. Sorry. You cannot return that. It's a sale item and all sales are final.

b. You can't return a sale item.

Activity 4   (Review transitions in *Destinations 1 Writing for Academic Success*—Unit 4, pp. 98–105.)

Decide if the question or request for each of the following situations is polite and appropriate. If it is, write a response to it. If it is not, write a new question and then a response to it.

1. Your sister is coming to visit you. Therefore, you want to pick her up at the airport today. You are asking your boss for permission to leave work early to get her at the airport.

    Can I leave work at 3:00 p.m. today to get my sister at the airport?

    _____

    _____

2. A new contract specialist is working at your office today. You want to ask her for some help with a computer problem.

    Come to my office before you leave today. I need help with a computer problem.

    _____

    _____

3. You are filling out an application for a new job in a reception area. However, your pen runs out of ink. You are asking the receptionist for a new pen.

    Give me another pen. This one is out of ink.

    _____

    _____

4. You need to get a box from the back of the top shelf. However, you cannot reach it. Another worker is next to you. You are asking this person to get the box for you.

    Would you get that box for me, please? I can't reach it.

    _____

    _____

5. You want to ask your boss about possibly changing your work situation because you want to advance in your career. You are asking to meet with her.

    Could we make an appointment to talk about my job?

    _____

    _____

Activity 5   (Review transitions in *Destinations 1 Writing for Academic Success*—Unit 4, pp. 98–105.)

Imagine you are in the following situations. Write a request for each situation using would/could/may/will/can *or an imperative. Then write an appropriate response. Make some of your responses positive and some negative.*

1. a. You are at a large company meeting with about 50 people in the room. The people in front of you are constantly talking. Therefore, it is difficult for you to hear the speaker. You cannot change seats. Ask these people to be quiet.

   _____

   b. These people did not pay attention to your first request. In other words, they are continuing to talk. Ask them to be quiet again.

   _____

2. a. You are in a reception area waiting for an interview for a new job. A large window is open, and the room is getting cold. Ask the receptionist to close the window.

   _____

   b. You are at work and the window is open. You are getting cold. Ask your friend to close the window.

   _____

   c. You are at home in your brother or sister's room, and the window is open. You are getting cold. Ask your brother or sister to close the window.

   _____

3. You are packing some boxes at work to be shipped out. However, you realize you don't have any tape to close up the box. Ask the following people for some tape.

   • the new employee working next to you
   • your good friend   • your supervisor

   _____

   _____

   _____

   _____

   _____

   _____

   _____

   _____

Suggestions and Advice

Should/Ought To/Had Better

Presentation

[1]Robert **should complete** his job application carefully.
[2]He **ought to answer** every question. [3]Therefore, he
should not leave any blank spaces on the paper.
[4]In addition, he **had better make** a good impression
on these papers in order to get an interview for the job.

Questions

1. Look at the bold words in sentences 1 and 2. What is the difference in the grammar of the bold words before the verbs?

2. Look at the bold words in sentence 3. What is the rule for making this sentence negative?

3. Read all three sentences. Do *should, ought to,* and *had better* all have exactly the same meaning? If not, how are they different?

Explanation—*Should/Ought To/Had Better*

1. We use *should, ought to,* and *had better* to make suggestions or give advice. The speaker (or writer) thinks something is a good idea.

   Should and *ought to* have basically the same meaning.

   > Robert *should* complete his application carefully.

   > Robert *ought to* complete his application carefully.

2. *Had better* is stronger than *should* and *ought to*. It can mean there is the possibility of a problem or a threat if someone does not follow the advice. *Had better* is more informal than the other two, and we use it mainly in speech.

   > Robert *had better* make a good impression on the application to get an interview. (If he does not make a good impression, he probably will not get an interview.)

   > Your boss says: You *had better* finish that report before 6 p.m. (If you don't, there could be a problem.)

3. a. *Should* follows all the grammar rules for modals as discussed on pages 146–147.

   > Robert *should complete* his job application carefully. He *should answer* every question.

   b. *Had better* also comes before the verb and does not make changes. Do not use *to* after the expression *had better*.

   > He *had better make* a good impression on his application.

   NOTE: *Had better* looks like it is in the past because of the word *had*. However, we do not use this expression for the past.

   Correct: He had better fill out the paper honestly. (present or future)

   He had better always tell the truth on his applications. (general/habitual time)

   Incorrect: He had better fill out the paper correctly yesterday. (past time)

   c. *Ought to* is different from *should* and *had better* because it requires *to* before the verb.

   > He *ought to answer* every question on the paper.

4. **Negative sentences**

   a. *Should*—Follow the rule for making a sentence negative.

   RULE: Add the word *not* after the auxiliary (helping verb).

   > Robert *should not (shouldn't*)* leave any blank spaces on the paper.

   > He *should not (shouldn't)* forget to answer some questions on the application.

Follow this pattern for negative sentences using *should:*

subject	auxiliary (helping verb)	not	verb (simple form)	
Robert	should	not	leave	any blank spaces on the paper.
He	should	not	forget	to answer some questions.

   b. *Had better*—We add the word *not* after both words of this expression.

   > He *had better not* be late for his interview.

   > She *had better not* give any incorrect information on her application.

---

*Native speakers often use contractions in conversation. We do not usually use these forms in formal writing.

Follow this pattern for negative sentences using *had better:*

subject	had better	not	verb (simple form)	
He	had better	not	be	late for his interview.
She	had better	not	give	any incorrect information on her application.

We do not usually use *ought to* in negative sentences.

5. **Questions—*Should***

We do not usually use *had better* and *ought to* in American English questions.

a. **Yes/No questions**

Place the auxiliary (helping verb) to the left of the subject of the sentence. End the sentence with a question mark.

Should she *answer* all the questions on the application?

Should he *be* on time for the job interview?

Follow this pattern for *yes/no* questions using *should:*

auxiliary (helping verb)	subject	verb (simple form)	
Should	she	answer	all the questions on the application?
Should	he	be	on time for the job interview?

b. **Question word questions**

Put the question word and the auxiliary (helping verb) to the left of the subject.

How should she *complete* the application?

When should she *arrive* for the job interview?

Follow this pattern for question word questions using *should:*

question word	auxiliary (helping verb)	subject	verb (simple form)	
How	should	she	complete	the application?
Why	should	she	apply	for that job?
When	should	she	arrive	for the job interview?
Where	should	the applicants	go	for the interview?
Who	should	*	be	at the interview at 3 p.m.?

*NOTE: Do not include a subject in these questions because the answer to *Who* is the subject.

6. **Pronunciation notes**

   a. Often people use a contraction with *had better.* When you hear these contractions in everyday speech, it may be difficult to hear the "d." (It may sound like "you better.")

      You'd better make a good impression on the application.

      He'd better answer all the questions.

   b. In conversation, *ought to* may sound like *oughtta.* You should never write this form, but you will hear native speakers use it in conversation.

Practice

Activity 1   (Review transitions in *Destinations 1 Writing for Academic Success*—Unit 4, pp. 98–105.)

A. *Circle the word or expression of advice or suggestion and the verb that follows it in these sentences.*

1. Each person ought to complete an application carefully and neatly.

2. The applicant should be honest with all of his answers. In other words, he had better not lie on the application.

3. The applicant ought to make sure the application is easy to read.

4. An application should look neat and clean. Therefore, an application had better not be too difficult to read.

B. *Put the letter of the answer to each question in the space provided.*

_____ 1. Should I use a pencil to fill out this application?

_____ 2. Should I use some *white out* to fix my mistakes on this application?

_____ 3. Where should I put my resume?

_____ 4. Should I answer every question?

_____ 5. What contact information should I give?

a. You should keep it together with the application in a folder.

b. Yes, you had better not leave any blank spaces, or the boss won't read it.

c. No, you had better start a new application.

d. You ought to include both your daytime phone number and email address.

e. No, you had better use a black or blue ink pen.

Activity 2

Circle the correct word or expression in parentheses. In some cases two answers may be correct. Circle both answers. Follow the example.

1. An applicant (should / (ought) / had better) to follow all instructions on an application.

2. You (should / ought) read all the instructions before filling out the application. In other words, you (ought / had better) show you can follow instructions.

3. An applicant (should / had better / ought) to include all his/her strong points and abilities on an application.

4. All applicants (should / ought to / had better) not write anything negative on an application.

5. The application (should not / had not better) be messy or difficult to read. This means an applicant (should not / ought not / had better not) erase answers.

6. You (ought / should / had better) to check the application for completeness before sending it.

 Activity 3

A. *Find and correct one mistake for each piece of advice below.*

Advice for people filling out a job application at an office:

1. You should to prepare a fact sheet about past jobs, including names and addresses of previous employers.

2. An applicant shoulds bring this paper to have all the correct information.

3. She ought to has information about references available as well.

4. Applicants had better to have the correct names and contact information for references.

5. They ought talk to their references before giving contact information on the application.

B.   Put a check (✔) next to each statement below that uses the expression had better *appropriately for the situation. If the use of* had better *is not appropriate for the situation, be prepared to explain why.*

_____ 1. (worker to supervisor)   You had better give me a raise.

_____ 2. (worker to good friend)   Yesterday you didn't do much work. You had better be more productive today.

_____ 3. (worker to new coworker)   The boss is very strict. You had better not be late for your appointment with the boss.

_____ 4. (supervisor to worker)   You had better complete that important report before the big meeting tomorrow.

_____ 5. (worker to coworker)   You had better share your lunch with me. I forgot mine at home.

Activity 4

Each of the following situations needs advice or a suggestion. Find an answer from the list below and write that answer in a complete sentence using should, ought to, *or* had better. *In one case you will make a negative answer. Use each answer from the list only one time.*

Answers:
a. be polite with the receptionist and take your time with the application
b. write "not applicable" or "does not apply" in those spaces
c. *(negative)* leave out any past job information
d. give all of your experience and accomplishments to be as competitive as possible
e. a daytime number so someone can answer any time

   EXAMPLE: What phone number is best for my application?

   You had better give a daytime number so someone can answer any time.

1. Do I need to write down all my past jobs on this application?

   _____

2. I am changing careers. Therefore, some questions do not relate to my past job experience.

   _____

3. Many people are applying for this job.

   _____

4. I'm a little nervous about going to an office to fill out an application.

   _____

Activity 5

For each situation write a sentence giving advice or a suggestion. Use should, ought to, *or* had better *in each of your answers. You may also give a negative answer.*

1. I forgot to write down the area code for my phone number on my application.

   _____

2. I think the boss from my last job will not give me a good recommendation.

   _____

3. I have an interview for a new job this afternoon, but I forget the name of the person to see.

   _____

4. I am not sure about the address to mail this application to.

   _____

5. I'm moving soon. What address is the best one to put on my application?

   _____

6. I lost my last job because of a bad situation. How should I answer the reason for leaving question on the application?

   _____

Necessity and Obligation

Must/Have To

Presentation 1

Questions

1. Look at the bold words in sentences 1 and 3. What is the meaning of the word *must* in those sentences?

2. Look at the bold words in sentences 2 and 4? Why does one use *have to* but the other *has to?*

3. Do *must* and *have to* mean the same thing?

[1]The workers in the bank **must dress** nicely for work. [2]For example, the men **have to wear** a tie every day. [3]Restaurant/factory workers **must wear** uniforms. [4]Each worker **has to be** sure the uniform is neat and clean each day.

Explanation—*Must/Have To*

1. Both *must* and *have to* express necessity or obligation.

   Those workers *must wear* a uniform.

   Those workers *have to wear* a uniform.

2. *Must* is a modal auxiliary (helping verb) and follows all the grammar rules for modals discussed on pages 146–147.

   Some workers *must wear* a tie to work.

   Other workers *must wear* a uniform.

3. The expression *have to* also comes before the verb, but it may change to fit the sentence. The verb after this expression does not add any endings.

    a. **Changes to fit the subject**

    Those workers *have to wear* a uniform.

    Each worker *has to wear* a uniform.

    b. **Changes to fit the time**

    He *has to wear* a tie to work every day.

    I *had to* wear a tie to work yesterday.

4. When *must* means obligation or necessity, we do not use it in the past. We use *had to* (the past of *have to*) to express past obligation or necessity.

    Correct: Yesterday he *had to* wear a tie to work.

    Incorrect: Yesterday he *must* wear a tie to work.

5. **Questions**

    We usually use *have to* for questions about obligation or necessity.

    a. *Yes/No questions with have to*

    To make *yes/no* questions with *have to,* put the auxiliary (helping verb) *do* before the subject.

    Do we *have to dress* nicely for that job?

    Does she *have to clean* her uniform often?

    If the sentence is in the future, use the auxiliary *will* and not the auxiliary *do.*

    Will he *have to wear* a tie to tomorrow's business meeting?

    (NOTE: See Unit 5 for more information about using *will* for future.)

    Follow this pattern for *yes/no* questions using *have to:*

auxiliary (helping verb)	subject	*have to + verb*	
Do	we	have to dress	nicely for that job?
Does	she	have to clean	her uniform often?
Did	you	have to buy	new clothes for your last job?
Will	he	have to wear	a tie to tomorrow's business meeting?

b. **Question word questions with *have to***

Put the question word and the auxiliary *do* to the left of the subject.

Why do they *have to wear* a tie to work?

When does he *have to wear* a tie for his job?

If the sentence is in the future, use the auxiliary *will* and not the auxiliary *do*.

When will she *have to get* a new uniform?

Follow this pattern for question word questions using *have to:*

question word	auxiliary (helping verb)	subject	*have to* + verb	
Why	do	they	have to wear	a tie to work?
Where	does	he	have to wear	a uniform?
When	will	she	have to get	a new uniform?
Where	did	you	have to buy	the uniform for that job?
Who*			has to**	wear a uniform to work?

*NOTE: Do not include a subject in these questions because the answer to *Who* is the subject.
**Always use *has to* for a question with *who.*

6. You may hear native speakers use *have to* more often than *must.*

In conversation, you may hear the following short forms. (You should never write these forms, but you will hear native speakers use them in conversation.)

- have to   You will hear *hafta.*
- has to   You will hear *hasta.*
- had to   You will hear *hadda.*

Practice

Activity 1

Read the following rules at a factory. Then fill in the left column of the chart with the subject of each sentence and the right column with a word or expression of necessity/obligation and the verb that follows it. Follow the example.

All employees must have proper identification while on the job.
- Every worker must wear a blue employee badge on the job. Each employee has to display this badge at all times.
- All visitors must take a red visitor's badge in the lobby. They also have to sign the visitor log at the reception desk. In addition, each visitor has to get permission to enter restricted areas.

subject	modal/expression + verb
employees	must have

Activity 2   (Review transitions in *Destinations 1 Writing for Academic Success*—Unit 4, pp. 98–105.)

A. *In the following company information for employees, circle the word or expression that fits each sentence. In some cases you should circle more than one answer. Follow the example.*

1. All new employees (have / (have to) / (must)) complete a physical exam before their first day of work. Therefore, each new employee (must / has to / have to) see a doctor for this.

2. (Do / Does / Is) each new employee (has to / have to / must) take a drug test at the time of hire? Yes. Furthermore, all workers (have / has / must) to take a drug test once a year.

3. Each newly hired worker (have / has / must) sign up for benefits with the Human Resources Department. For example, all employees (must / has to / have to) sign papers for health insurance there.

4. All employees (must / have to / has to) follow the company holiday schedule. In addition, every worker (must / have / has) to work the day before and the day after a holiday unless she/he gets special permission from a supervisor.

B. *Circle the correct word or expression in parentheses in the following conversation.*

New worker: (Do / Does / Must) employees fill out any papers for vacation
              1

              days in this company?

Coworker: You (have / has / must) to hand in a vacation request
              2

              form at least two weeks in advance. Last year we

              (have to /must / had to) hand that in just one week before.
              3

              However, this year they changed the rules. Also, everyone

              (must / have to / has) turn in his/her requests on time.
              4

New worker: Do we (must / have to / had to) call on a sick day?
              5

Coworker: Yes, all employees (must / has / have) to call their
              6

              direct supervisor when they are sick. In addition, you

              (must / have to / has to) bring a note from the doctor after
              7

              three days of sick pay.

Activity 3

A. *Add the word or expression in parentheses and one of the verbs from the list to each sentence. Use each verb only one time. Follow the example.*

wear	wake up	remember	stay	work	take

1. George (must) _____*must work*_____ every Thursday night and
    Saturday morning.

2. Paula (have to) _____ at the office until 8 p.m.
    every Monday.

3. They both (have to) _____ nice clothes to work.

4. George (have to) _____ at 6 a.m. in order to get to
    work on time.

5. Paula (must) _____ a business trip once a month
    for her job.

6. Both Paula and George (must) _____ to wear their
    badges at the office.

B. *Using the expression* have to, *rewrite sentences 1–3 in the past about their jobs last year.*

_____

_____

_____

C. *Using the expression* have to *rewrite sentences 4–6 as yes/no questions.*

_____

_____

_____

Presentation 2

a

b

[1]These workers **must wear** uniforms at work. [2]They **must not come** to the job in everyday street clothes.

[3]These workers usually **have to wear** nicer clothes to work. [4]However, today is "casual Friday," so they **do not have to follow** the usual rules.

Questions

1. What is the meaning of *must* and *have to* in sentences 1 and 3?

2. Is the meaning of *must not* in sentence 2 the same as the meaning of *do not have to* in sentence 4?

Explanation—Negatives: *Must Not* and *Don't Have To*

1. a. To make negative sentences with *must* and *have to* follow the rule for making a sentence negative.

    RULE: Add the word *not* after the auxiliary (helping verb).

    Those workers *must not (mustn't)** *come* to the job in everyday street clothes.

    You *must not (mustn't)** *wear* jeans and a t-shirt to work.

_____

*Contractions are often used in conversation. They are not usually used in formal writing.

Follow this pattern for negative sentences using *must:*

subject	auxiliary (helping verb)	not	verb (simple form)	
They	must	not	come	to the job in everyday street clothes.
You	must	not	wear	jeans and a t-shirt to work.

b. To make a negative sentence with *have to,* add *not* after the helping verb (auxiliary) *do.*

They *do not (don't)** have to follow* the rules on "casual Friday."

My friend *does not (doesn't)** have to* arrive at work before 9:00 a.m.

He *did not (didn't)** have to* buy a new uniform for his job.

If the sentence is in the future, use the auxiliary *will* and not the auxiliary *do.*

He *will not (won't)** have to buy / wear* specific clothing for his new job.

Follow this pattern for negative sentences using *have to:*

subject	auxiliary (helping verb)	not	*have to +* verb	
They	do	not	have to follow	the rules on "casual Friday."
My friend	does	not	have to arrive	at work before 9:00 a.m.
He	did	not	have to buy	a new uniform for his job.
He	will	not	have to wear	specific clothing for his new job.

2. *Must not* has a strong meaning. It says that something is not allowed or it is prohibited. It involves a rule or requirement, and there is no choice in this situation.

They *must not wear* jeans and a t-shirt to work. (Jeans and a t-shirt are not allowed on that job.)

You *must not smoke* in the building. (This is a rule or a law. Smoking is not allowed.)

3. The negative forms of *have to* are not as strong. They indicate that something is not necessary, and there is a choice.

You *don't have to follow* the usual rules on "casual Friday." (This is your choice. You can follow the clothing rules if you like, but it is not necessary.)

My friend *doesn't have to arrive at work* before 9:00 a.m. (This is her choice. She can arrive at work before 9:00 a.m. or not.)

---

*Contractions are often used in conversation. They are not usually used in formal writing.

Practice

Activity 4   (Review transitions in *Destinations 1 Writing for Academic Success*—Unit 4, pp. 98–105.)

Write the letter of the sentence on the right that follows each sentence on the left.

_____ 1. The process of retrieving your voice mail requires several steps.

_____ 2. You will need a password each time you want to retrieve your messages.

_____ 3. The password requires at least 3 letters. However, you can also choose numbers.

_____ 4. The phone system is interactive.

_____ 5. It is important to wait for the instructions.

a. Thus, you must set up your password immediately.

b. In other words, the user has to respond to the instructions on the system.

c. Therefore, you have to follow all these instructions carefully.

d. For instance, the user must not give a password before the recording asks for it.

e. In other words, you don't have to choose letters exclusively.

Activity 5   (Review transitions in *Destinations 1 Writing for Academic Success*—Unit 4, pp. 98–105.)

Find nine mistakes in the following information about changing a cartridge in a printer. Most of the mistakes are about grammar, but one is about meaning. Not every sentence has a mistake.

1. Changing a print cartridge is not the same for all machines. For one thing, on some printers you must to press the *on* button to open the cover. However, for other printers you not have to push the *on* button.

2. The cartridge is inside the printer. Therefore, you has to open the door to get to the cartridge.

3. There is usually a cover over the cartridge. In this case the user must lifts the cover.

4. An ink cartridge cannot work properly with the pink tab on it. As a result, the user have to remove that tab.

5. Touching the copper-colored contacts on a cartridge can cause a problem. In other words, you must not to touch those contacts.

6. The cartridge only fits in the slot with the label on the top. Therefore, you don't have to put it in upside down.

7. The printer will not work with the access door open, so you must forget not to close the door.

8. Finally, each user musts pay attention to any other instructions on the door of the printer.

Activity 6   (Review coordinating conjunctions: Unit 3, pages 66–75 and transitions: Unit 4, pp. 98–105 in *Destinations 1 Writing for Academic Success.*)

A.   *Fill in the following spaces with* must not, don't have to, *or* doesn't have to.

1. Joanna and Paula work at an office on a job share system. In other words, they _____ come to work on the
   _a
   same days. Therefore, they _____ forget to
   _b
   communicate with each other often about their work.

2. Employees at Steve's factory work staggered hours. For instance, Steve works from 8:00 a.m. to 5:00 p.m., but his coworker, Gloria, _____ arrive until 10:00 a.m.

3. Cindy telecommutes for her job, so she works at home. Sometimes it's difficult for her to get all her work done, but she _____ get behind in her work. She
   _a
   _____ follow a strict working schedule
   _b
   at home. However, she _____ spend
   _c
   too much time on other things.

B.   *Fill in each space with* must, have to, *or* has to. *Use the negative form where indicated.*

There is a very specific procedure for packing a product for shipment. Each employee _____ follow all the rules and does not have any options to change them.

1. There are preprinted shipping labels in order to make sure the address is correct. Therefore, you *(negative)* _____ make any new labels.

2. Each carton requires one dozen bags of the product. In other words, you *(negative)* _____ pack fewer than twelve bags in a box.

3. Each carton will go on a shipping pallet. The pallets are very heavy. Therefore, warehouse workers _____ move those
a
with a forklift. In other words, you *(negative)* _____
b
move the pallets into the warehouse by yourself.

4. You _____ cover the product with packing material in
a
each box because you *(negative)* _____ leave the
b
product unprotected. Three ounces of packing material is usually a good amount, but it *(negative)* _____ be this exact amount.
c
Therefore, you *(negative)* _____ measure the packing
d
material exactly.

Activity 7

Advertisements for job openings describe the job and discuss the skills and/or abilities an applicant needs. When a skill is necessary, they often say it is "a must" or "necessary." When a skill is recommended but not necessary, they often say it is "a plus."'

A. *Below you will find two advertisements for job openings in the United States. Read each one and discuss any new vocabulary or abbreviations that you don't understand.*

❶
CLERICAL
P-T Bilingual position (Eng/Spa)
Busy office – must have good
telephone skills
2 years exp in office work required,
with more than two a plus
Must know MS Office. Knowledge of
Quickbooks recommended.
Hours: M–F 9:00-1:00
Call for an appointment 619-555-8033

❷
DRIVERS WANTED
Mostly night shift but some
day shifts available.
Must have clean DMV record
and current driver's license.
Your own pickup truck,
minivan, or cargo van a plus
Call: 800-533-8088 ext 53

B. Now decide what skills are necessary and what skills are recommended.
    List these skills for each advertisement.

A must (necessary)	A plus (recommended)
1.	
2.	

C. Write at least three sentences about requirements for either or both of the
    jobs on page 180. Then write three sentences about recommended skills for
    these jobs. Use must *and* have to *in your sentences about the requirements.*
    Use should, ought to, *and* don't have to *in your sentences about the*
    recommendations.

Requirements

1. _____

    _____

2. _____

    _____

3. _____

    _____

Recommendations

1. _____

    _____

2. _____

    _____

3. _____

    _____

Possibility and Probability

May/Might/Could/Must

Presentation 1

Questions

1. What do the words in bold in sentences 1 and 2 mean? Are these strong words or weak in meaning?

2. What is the time in each of the sentences?

[1]These people **might** be at a meeting. [2]They **may** all work for the same company, or one of them **could** be a consultant. [3]They **might not finish** until late tonight.

Explanation—*May/Might/Could*

1. The modals *could*, *may*, and *might* indicate possibility. We use these modals when we are not sure about a situation and want to give the meaning of *perhaps* or *maybe*.

   Those people *might be* at a meeting.

   They *may* all *work* for the same company.

2. These three words follow all the grammar rules for modals discussed on pages 146–147.

   One of them *could be* a consultant.

   The meeting *might* continue for a long time.

3. **Negative sentences—***may* and *might*

   Follow the rule for making a sentence negative.

   RULE: Add the word *not* after the auxiliary (helping verb).

   They *might not finish* until late tonight.

   He *may not work* at that company.

Follow this pattern for negative sentences using *may* and *might*:

subject	auxiliary (helping verb)	not	verb (simple form)	
They	might	not	finish	until late tonight.
He	may	not	work	at that company.

NOTE: We do not use *could* in negative sentences for the meaning of perhaps or maybe. *Could not* says that something is impossible or almost impossible. It is stronger than *may not* and *might not* when negative.

My friend got a 25 percent raise in her salary last week.

That *couldn't be* true. (It seems impossible.)

4. **Questions**

   For the meaning of perhaps or maybe, we usually use only the word *could* in questions.

   a. *Yes/No questions*

      Place the auxiliary (helping verb) to the left of the subject of the sentence. End the sentence with a question mark.

      Could that man *be* a freelance consultant?

      Could you *try* to end the meeting soon?

Follow this pattern for *yes/no* questions using *could:*

auxiliary (helping verb)	subject	verb (simple form)	
Could	that man	be	a freelance consultant?
Could	you	try	to end the meeting soon?

   b. **Question word questions**

      Put the question word and the auxiliary to the left of the subject.

      Where could we *meet* to discuss the report?

      When could you *finish* that project?

      Why could we *lose* our extra pay?

Follow this pattern for question word questions using *could:*

question word	auxiliary (helping verb)	subject	verb (simple form)	
Where	could	we	meet	to discuss the report?
When	could	you	finish	that project?
Why	could	we	lose	our extra pay?

5. We use *could*, *may*, and *might* to indicate possibility in both present and future situations.

> Those people *could be* in a meeting. They *might finish* in a few minutes.

> The company *may be* ready to give the workers a raise.

> The boss *might announce* this tomorrow.

> We *could get* new options for our benefits. We *may hear* about this next week.

6. Do not confuse the words *may be* (two words) with *maybe* (one word).

may + be = modal auxiliary + verb

> The ink cartridge *may be* in the box under the table.

Maybe is not a verb. It is an adverb and is often at the beginning of a sentence.

> *Maybe* the ink cartridge is in a box under the table, or *maybe* it fell under the desk.

Practice

Activity 1

A. On the line given next to each number, write the situation that fits the possibilities under the line.

B. Circle all the modals of possibility and the verbs that follow them in these sentences.

Situations: Teresa is on the phone in her office with the door closed.
Yumi seems nervous right now.
The printer for my computer is not working.

1. _____
   a. She could be on her way to an interview for a new job.
   b. She might be ready for her big presentation at today's meeting.
   c. She may have a performance review meeting with her supervisor today.

2. _____
   a. It may require a change in settings on your computer.
   b. It might not be plugged in.
   c. It could need a new ink cartridge.

3. _____
   a. The call might involve an important business deal.
   b. She could need some privacy right now.
   c. It may not be a business call.

Activity 2

The people in the following sentences are looking for a new job. Complete each sentence by adding a modal of possibility (may, might, or could) and a verb from the list. Some spaces may have more than one possible answer, but you should use each verb only one time. Use each of the modals at least once in your answers. Follow the example.

| VERBS: look   go   search   take   contact   ask   check |

1. Mark _____ may look _____ in the want ad section of the newspaper.

2. Selena _____ some friends about openings at their jobs.

3. Thi _____ to an employment agency for jobs in her field.

4. Hamid _____ the job board at his school's Career Center.

5. Sylvia _____ several people from her old job.

6. Corey _____ a quick look at a job search site on the

   Internet. Then he _____ the websites of the individual

   companies with openings more carefully.

Activity 3

Add the idea of maybe or perhaps by adding may, could, *or* might *to each sentence. Rewrite each sentence including the modal in the space provided. If the original sentence is negative, be sure your sentence is negative as well. Use all three modals at least once.*

   EXAMPLE: Joe works on Saturdays to get overtime pay.

   Joe may (OR might OR could) work on Saturdays to get overtime pay.

1. I want to look for a new job.

   _____

2. That man is the supervisor of the Shipping Department.

   _____

3. That company offers a good benefits package.

   _____

4. Amir doesn't have Sundays off at his new job.

   _____

5. We plan to take a week's vacation in August.

   _____

6. The new employee doesn't get a full week of vacation this year.

   _____

¹These men **must be** at a construction site. ²The man on the left is wearing a tie and looking at plans. ³He **must work** as a supervisor or architect. ⁴He **must not be** a construction worker.

Presentation 2

Questions

1. Look at the word *must* in sentences 1 and 3. Do you think this modal means obligation or necessity in these sentences?

   What is the meaning of the word *must* in these sentences?

2. How do we make a sentence negative using the word *must* with this meaning?

Explanation—Using *Must* for Probability

1. Sometimes we have a limited amount of information about something. Using this information, we can make a conclusion about the person or situation. We often use the modal *must* to make this conclusion.

2. In Presentation 1 of this lesson, you learned about words that show possibility *(could/might/may)*. In some cases you might use these words for conclusions, but they are not as strong as *must* for this meaning. We use *must* to say we think something is probably true.

25%	50%	90–95%

   not sure/possibly = might/could/may—25%   more sure/probably = must—90–95%

   a. She is not answering her telephone. She *could/may/might be* out of the office. (possibility—She might also be at a meeting or on a break.)

   b. The plane was due to arrive in Chicago at 5:00 p.m., but it's 5:15 p.m., and it is still not there. The plane *must be* late. (We don't know this for sure, but we think it could easily be true. In other words, there is a strong possibility that this is true.)

3. **Negative sentences with *must* as a conclusion**

   You *must not be* happy at your new job because you are already looking for a new one.

   She is at work today, so she *must not feel* too sick to go out of the house.

   Follow the rule for making a sentence negative.

   RULE: Add the word *not* after the auxiliary (helping verb).

Follow this pattern for negative sentences using *must:*

subject	auxiliary (helping verb)	not	verb (simple form)	
You	must	not	be	happy with your new job.
She	must	not	feel	too sick to go to work.

NOTE: Do not use the contraction *(mustn't)* in a negative conclusion using *must.*

Practice

Activity 4

A. *Write the piece of information from the list below that fits each sentence. Then circle the modal and the verb that follows it. Use each piece of information only one time.*

compressed work week	job sharing	virtual environment
telecommuter	core hours	freelance specialist

1. Bob does not work for only one company. In other words, he has contracts with several different companies. He must work as a

   _____.

2. Brianna's workweek consists of four ten-hour workdays, Monday through Thursday. She must have a _____.

3. Employees at that company work staggered hours of 7:00 a.m. to 4:00 p.m. and 9:00 a.m. to 6:00 p.m. The _____ must be from 9:00 a.m. to 4:00 p.m.

4. Tina and Chris work the same job as office clerk for the Human Resources Department. Tina works mornings only and Chris works afternoons only. Their company must allow _____.

5. Sara usually works at home in a _____. She must not see her coworkers in the office very much. She must be a

   _____.

B. *Fill in each blank space with a conclusion using the modal* must *and the verb in parentheses. Make the sentence negative if indicated.*

1. Maria wears a postal worker's uniform. She (work)

   _____ for the postal service.

2. George called and said he is on his way to work, but he's not here yet.

   He (be) _____ caught in heavy traffic.

3. John is asking his coworker to borrow some money for lunch. John

   (have–*negative*) _____ enough money to

   buy lunch.

4. Sally is greeting the owner of the company and having a conversation

   with him. She (know) _____ him.

Activity 5

In some of the following sentences must *means obligation or necessity. However, in other sentences it means a conclusion. Put the letter* C *next to each sentence that indicates a conclusion.*

1. In the United States everyone must pay taxes and file tax returns
   by April 15th.

2. Bill's boss says he must finish his report immediately.

3. Jose is not answering emails today. He must not need to check
   his mail.

4. That young boy with the red hair must be the owner's son.

5. You must fill out a time sheet in order to get paid.

6. You must be tired after staying at the meeting until 11:00 p.m.
   last night.

7. Yuko must get to her office by 8:00 a.m. tomorrow in order to be
   on time for the meeting.

8. You must be very happy about getting that big raise last week.

9. You must provide references on your application for this job.

Activity 6

Write a sentence that expresses a conclusion based on the information given.
Use the modal must *and the words in parentheses in each answer.*

EXAMPLE: Joe buys a new Mercedes every year. (a lot of money)

He (Joe) must have a lot of money.   *OR* He must earn a lot of money.

1. It's 11:30 a.m. Therefore, everyone's going to the cafeteria.
   (be lunch time)

   _____

2. Claudia and Nadia work in the same department of that company.
   (know each other)

   _____

3. That woman is showing her identification badge to the security guard.
   (be a visitor)

   _____

4. Those people are looking at a map of the building and talking about it.
   (be lost)

   _____

5. That man leaves that office building every day at 5 p.m. (work there)

   _____

6. Those two workers are communicating in sign language.
   (be hearing impaired)

   _____

7. An office worker is reading an instruction booklet and pulling out papers
   from the photocopier. (have a paper jam)

   _____

8. The customer is taking his credit card out of his wallet.
   (want pay the bill)

   _____

Activity 7

Answer the following questions about the photos below. Be sure to use the modals about possibility (can/might/could) *and probability* (must) *from this lesson in your answers.*

A

B

1. Who are these people?

2. Where are they?

3. Why are they there?

4. How do you think the people in these pictures feel?

_____

_____

_____

_____

_____

_____

_____

_____

Future—Will

Predictions/Intentions/Offers

[1]She is getting information about a distance education class, and she **will take** a hybrid accounting class next semester. [2]She **will be** successful in this type of class because she telecommutes for her job and loves to do work on computers.

Presentation

Questions

1. Look at the words in bold in both sentences. What word do you see before the verb?

2. Do you see any endings (such as *-s* or *-ed*) on any of the words in bold? What is the time in these sentences? How do you know this?

3. What is the meaning of *will* in each of these sentences?

Explanation—*Will* for Predictions, Intentions, Offers

1. *Will* is a modal auxiliary (helping verb) and follows all the grammar rules about modals. (See Unit 4, pp. 146–147 for a review of these rules.)

2. We use *will* as follows:

   a. To make a prediction about something in the future. A prediction announces something before it happens.

      She *will be* successful in this type of class because she telecommutes for her job and loves to do work on computers.

      Some people *will take* an online class because it is convenient for their schedules.

   Sometimes we also use the word *probably* in these predictions. We usually put the word *probably* between *will* and the verb.

      She *will probably* be successful in this type of class.

      Some people *will probably take* an online class because it is convenient for their schedules.

b. **To state an intention or plan**—Often this is something a person decides at the moment of speaking or at the time something is taking place.

Student: That online accounting class is almost full.

Friend: Thanks for telling me. *I'll* register* for it today.

Sometimes this may be an offer to do something.

I ca*n't** find the discussion board for this class.

I'll* help you.

3. **Negative sentences**—Follow the rule for making a sentence negative.

RULE: Add the word *not* after the auxiliary (helping verb).

She *will not (won't*) register* for any other classes in addition to the hybrid class.

The class *will not (won't*) meet* face-to-face more than three times this semester.

Follow this pattern for negative sentences using *will:*

subject	auxiliary (helping verb)	not	verb (simple form)	
She	will	not	register	for any other classes.
The class	will	not	meet	face-to-face more than three times this semester.

4. **Questions**—Follow the rule for making questions.

RULE: Move the auxiliary to the left of the subject of the sentence.

a. *Yes/No questions*

Will she *succeed* in that class?

Will they *register* for any other classes?

Follow this pattern for yes/no questions using *will:*

auxiliary (helping verb)	subject	verb (simple form)	
Will	she	succeed	in that class?
Will	they	register	for any other classes?

b. **Question word questions**

When will she *register* for that class?

How will he *succeed* in that class?

---

*Contractions are often used in conversation. They are not usually used in formal writing.

Put the question word and the auxiliary (helping verb) to the left of the subject to make the sentence a question.

Follow this pattern for question word questions using *will*:

question word	auxiliary (helping verb)	subject	verb (simple form)	
When	will	she	register	for that class?
How	will	you	succeed	in that class?
Who	will	*	pass	the class?

*NOTE: Do not include a subject in these questions because the answer to *Who* is the subject.

5. Time words and expressions that indicate future time:

- next week/month/year/Monday/March, etc.
- in three hours/days/weeks
- tonight/later/tomorrow
- two days/weeks/months from now

You may not always see time words or expressions with *will*. This is because we know that the time is future from the meaning of the word.

Practice

Activity 1   (Review subordinating conjunctions in *Destinations 1 Writing for Academic Success*—Unit 5, pp. 127–138.)

A. *Write the letter of the response on the right to each statement on the left. Use each response only one time. Then circle will and the verb following it in each of the responses.*

_____ 1. There are only two seats left in the hybrid English reading class.

_____ 2. Because I don't have access to the Internet today, I can't sign up for the class.

_____ 3. I'm having trouble understanding the new assignment.

_____ 4. I can't install this new program on my computer.

_____ 5. We have a deadline to participate on the discussion board by 6 p.m.

a. No problem. I'll let you use my laptop to enroll.

b. I'll do that right now because I have to work all afternoon.

c. I'll do that for you. I know that application.

d. I'll register for it this afternoon.

e. I'll help you. Maybe we can form a study group.

B. *Look back at the responses and decide if each one is an offer or an intention/decision.*

W   *Activity 2*   (Review subordinating conjunctions in *Destinations 1 Writing for Academic Success*—Unit 5, pp. 127–138.)

A. *Circle* will + *verb in each of the following predictions, intentions/decisions, and offers.*

B. *In the space provided next to each number, label each sentence as follows:*

I = intention/decision   O = offer   P = prediction

EXAMPLE: __P__   John will do well in his online class because he loves to use his computer.

_____ 1. More working students will take online classes in the next year or two because they like the flexibility.

_____ 2. The instructor just posted today's assignment on the Internet. I'll check it this afternoon.

_____ 3. I can't access the chat room for my online biology class. I'll help you do that in a few minutes.

_____ 4. There's an interesting speaker coming to school tonight, but I don't want to see her by myself. I'll go with you.

_____ 5. People will enroll in more hybrid classes in the future.

_____ 6. The teacher offered an assignment for extra credit on the assignment board today. I'll do that tonight because I need the extra points for my grade.

Activity 3   (Review subordinating conjunctions in *Destinations 1 Writing for Academic Success*—Unit 5, pp. 127–138.)

A.   *Fill in the following predictions with a verb from the list below. Use each verb only one time.*

B.   *Circle* will *or* will not *for each prediction. Follow the example.*

| be | take | do | think | enroll | have | enjoy |

1.   Patti needs flexibility because she has a changing work schedule. She
     ((will)/ will not) _____take_____ an online class this semester.

2.   Joann does not have easy access to the Internet because she only uses
     the computers at the library. She (will / will not) _____ in a
     distance education class.

3.   Bill does not know much about computers and needs help with email
     and the Internet. An online class (will / will not) _____ a good
     choice for him.

4.   Galina likes using the Internet and sending email messages. She
     (will / will not) _____ an online class.

5.   Raul is not a very independent worker because he needs help
     completing reports and projects. He (will / will not) _____
     a lot of success in an online class.

6.   Cara usually completes all her assignments early. She (will / will not)
     _____ well in an online class.

7.   Stuart thinks that working with classmates face-to-face is very important.
     He (will / will not) _____ about taking an online class.

Activity 4 (Review subordinating conjunctions in *Destinations 1 Writing for Academic Success*—Unit 5, pp. 127–138.)

Find and correct six mistakes in the following email messages.

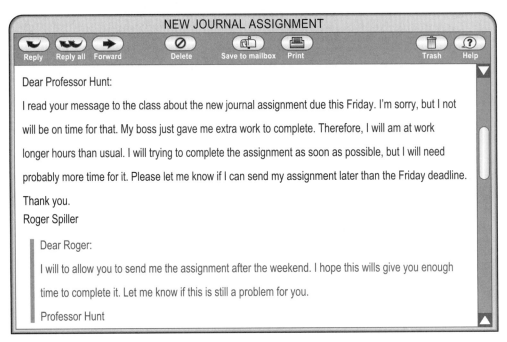

NEW JOURNAL ASSIGNMENT

Reply   Reply all   Forward   Delete   Save to mailbox   Print   Trash   Help

Dear Professor Hunt:

I read your message to the class about the new journal assignment due this Friday. I'm sorry, but I not will be on time for that. My boss just gave me extra work to complete. Therefore, I will am at work longer hours than usual. I will trying to complete the assignment as soon as possible, but I will need probably more time for it. Please let me know if I can send my assignment later than the Friday deadline.

Thank you.
Roger Spiller

Dear Roger:

I will to allow you to send me the assignment after the weekend. I hope this wills give you enough time to complete it. Let me know if this is still a problem for you.

Professor Hunt

Activity 5

A. *Using the information given under each line, write a question. Do not add or take out any words.*

B. *After you write all the questions, ask a classmate each one. Write his/her answers on the lines given.*

1. _____?

   you / enroll in / a hybrid course / will / next semester

   Answer: _____

2. _____?

   feel comfortable / you / next year / will / taking / an online class in English

   Answer: _____

3. _____?

   take / will / how many / at this school / you / non-degree classes

   Answer: _____

4. _____ ?

next semester's classes / when / you / will / register for

Answer: _____

5. _____ ?

will / complete your work/ where / for the online class / you

Answer: _____

Activity 6

Read each of the following situations and write a prediction, intention/decision, or offer by following the instructions given for each one. Write complete sentences using will.

1. You are taking a new online course, and the instructor just gave the first assignment from the textbook. Your friend is taking the same course, but she cannot get to the bookstore to buy the book today. Make an offer to help her.

   _____

2. Write a prediction about each of the following people taking an online course. Your answers may be negative or positive predictions.

   a. Greg is shy, and he does not like to go to other people for help, especially instructors.

   _____

   b. Marta feels very comfortable reading and writing in English. She cannot get to school easily because she does not drive.

   _____

3. You are talking to a counselor at school, and he wants you to decide about taking an online course over the summer. Tell him your decision.

   _____

Future—Be Going To/ *Present Progressive*

Predictions/Plans/Expectations

Presentation 1

Questions

1. What is the time of the caption to this picture? How do you know this? What specific words tell you the time?

2. What form of the verb follows the expression *(be) going to* in each sentence? (Do you see any endings on the verbs that follow this expression?)

3. What is the meaning of the expression *(be) going to* in sentence 1 and sentence 3?

[1]Suzie **is going to** spend all night on her class assignment tonight. [2]She **is not going to** stop working because she needs to finish it by tomorrow's deadline. [3]She **is probably going to** get an A on this paper.

Explanation—*Be Going To* for Predictions, Plans, Expectations

1. In Lesson 27 you learned about using *will* for predictions and intentions/offers. We also use the expression *be going to* to talk about the future.

2. To use *be going to* + verb, follow these rules:

   a. Be sure to have all three words *(be going to)* before the verb.

   b. Change the *be* in this expression to agree with the subject.

c. Make sure to keep the verb after the word *to* in simple form (no endings such as *-s* or *-ed*).

Suzie *is going to spend* all night on the class assignment tonight.

1   2   3   verb

All of the students *are going to spend* all night on the class assignment tonight. 1   2   3   verb

3. **Negative sentences**—Follow the rule for making a sentence negative.

RULE: Add the word *not* after the auxiliary (helping verb) *be.*

Suzie *is not (isn't*)* going to spend all night on the assignment tonight.

Her classmates *are not (aren't*)* going to spend all night on the assignment tonight.

Follow this pattern for negative sentences using *be going to:*

subject	auxiliary (helping verb)	not	*going to* + verb	
Suzie	is	not	going to spend	all night on the assignment tonight.
Her classmates	are	not	going to spend	all night on the assignment tonight.

4. **Questions**—Follow the rule for making questions.

RULE: Move *be* to the left of the subject of the sentence.

a. *Yes/No* **questions**

Is Suzie *going to* spend all night on the assignment tonight?

Are her classmates *going to* spend all night on the assignment tonight?

Follow this pattern for *yes/no* questions using *be going to:*

auxiliary (helping verb)	subject	*going to* + verb	
Is	Suzie	going to spend	all night on the assignment tonight?
Are	her classmates	going to spend	all night on the assignment tonight?

b. **Question word questions**

When is Suzie *going to* complete that assignment?

How are they *going to* help her?

Put the question word and the auxiliary to the left of the subject to make the sentence a question.

---

*Contractions are often used in conversation. They are not usually used in formal writing.

Follow this pattern for question word questions using *be going to:*

question word	auxiliary (helping verb)	subject	*going to* + verb	
When	is	Suzie	going to complete	that assignment?
How	are	they	going to help	her?
Why	are	they	going to take	a hybrid class?
Who	is	*	going to take	that class?

*NOTE: Do not include a subject in these questions because the answer to *Who* is the subject.

5. We use *be going to* as follows:

    a. To make a prediction about something in the future.

        She *is going to get* an A on that assignment.

        All of the students *are going to* pass that class.

        Sometimes we also use the word *probably* in these predictions. We usually put the word *probably* between *be* and *going to*.

        She *is probably going to* get an A on that assignment.

        All of the students *are probably going to* pass that class.

    b. To talk about plans for the future.

        She *is going to* finish the classes for her major online because those classes fit her schedule.

        Joe and Cindy *are going to* take two hybrid classes next summer.

    c. To express an expectation or result.

        Sometimes we may have an expectation about the very near future. We expect a certain result from something we see or know about the present.

        EXAMPLE: The printing is very light on this paper, so I can hardly read it.

        (expectation) The printer *is going to* run out of ink very soon.

6. Time words and expressions that indicate future time:

    *   next week/month/year/Monday/March, etc.
    *   in three hours/days/weeks
    *   tonight/later/tomorrow
    *   two days/weeks/months from now

    You may not always see time words or expressions with *be going to*. This is because we know that the time is future from the meaning of the expression.

Practice

Activity 1

Circle the expression (be) going to *and the verb wherever it appears in the following sentences. Then answer the questions that follow these sentences.*

1. a. I loved my hybrid class last semester.

    b. Next semester I am going to make my entire schedule online classes.

2. a. Joe finished almost all of the required classes for his major.

    b. He's going to take the remaining ones through distance education.

3. a. We're going to participate in a real time discussion for our history class this afternoon.

    b. Most of the students are probably going to review all the chapters in the book before the discussion.

4. a. Your laptop is too big for that space on the desk.

    b. It's going to fall off the desk.

5. a. Devices such as GPS systems are probably going to become cheaper and more popular in the next few years.

    b. More people will own them.

 Questions

a. Which one sentence above is an expectation?

b. Which two sentences are plans?

c. Which three sentences are predictions?

Activity 2 (Review subordinating conjunctions in *Destinations 1 Writing for Academic Success*—Unit 5, pp. 127–138.)

Complete each sentence by writing the letter on the right that fits. Use each letter only one time.

_____ 1. Guillermo is going to buy a computer

_____ 2. Alicia is going to take one or two hybrid classes next semester

_____ 3. Because Jim is not comfortable using computers,

_____ 4. Phil is probably going to enjoy his online classes because

_____ 5. Because Cindy needs to improve her reading skills,

_____ 6. Because the battery is low on my laptop,

a. he is not going to enroll in any hybrid classes.

b. because he wants to try an online class.

c. it's going to shut off automatically soon.

d. she is not going to take an online class this semester.

e. because she doesn't have time to come to campus too many times a week.

f. he loves to work independently at home.

Activity 3 (Review subordinating conjunctions in *Destinations 1 Writing for Academic Success*—Unit 5, pp. 127–138.)

Fill in each of the spaces using be going to *and the word or words in parentheses. Follow the example. Be sure to make your answers in Part B negative.*

A. Carol's hybrid political science class meets once a week at school, and

tomorrow's class (cover) ___*is going to cover*___ some difficult

₁

information. She (prepare) _____ for that

₂

class this evening because she has to work tomorrow morning. She

(probably study) _____ at the library after her

₃

class to get ahead for the following week. Her classmates Bill and Arlene

(meet) _____ to study together in the morning.

₄

They (probably join) _____ Carol at the library

₅

after class.

B. Barbara (enroll–*negative*) _____ in an

₁

online class because she uses her computer for recreation only.

She (try—probably–*negative*) _____ to

₂

use her computer for school because she (have–*negative*)

_____ time to learn more about using

₃

her computer.

Presentation 2

¹Suzie **is meeting** her classmates at a coffee shop tomorrow morning to prepare their group project. ²Tomorrow afternoon they **are sending** their work online through email for a grade.

Questions

1. Circle the words in bold in sentence 1 and sentence 2. Circle any time words in those two sentences.

2. What is the time of these sentences? How do you know this?

Explanation—Using Present Progressive for Plans

1. In Unit 1, Lesson 6, you learned about using present progressive verb forms for present time. Native speakers often use these verb forms for future time also, especially in conversation or informal writing.

2. When you use these forms for future time, be sure to use future time words or expressions. You need these words and expressions to be sure the future time is clear.

   a. Suzie is meeting her classmates at a coffee shop to prepare their group project. Is this right now or at a future time?

   b. They are submitting their work online for a grade. Is this right now or at a future time?

   Without more information, we cannot be sure about the time in sentences *a* and *b*.

(For a review of negative sentences and questions with present progressive verb forms, see Unit 1, Lessons 6 and 7.)

Practice

Activity 4

Indicate the time of each sentence as P *for present or* F *for future on the line next to the letter. Then underline the verb and any time words in each sentence. Follow the example.*

____P____ 1. a. My friend <u>is taking</u> an online non-degree course <u>this semester</u>.

_____   b. Next semester he is enrolling in a three-unit hybrid reading course.

_____ 2. a. Raul is participating in an online seminar for his job this month.

_____   b. His company is sending him to a special seminar about using computers next month.

_____ 3. a. Today Belinda is posting some comments on the online forum for her business class.

_____   b. Tomorrow her class is meeting face-to-face because the students are presenting their final projects.

Activity 5

In the following online discussion between two students, find eight mistakes and correct them.

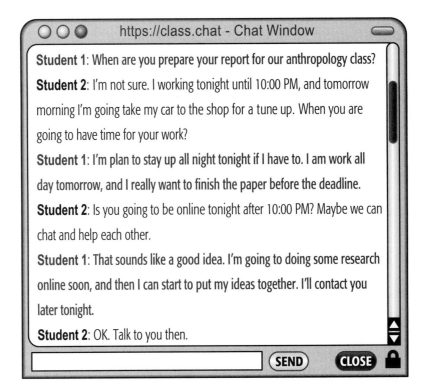

Student 1: When are you prepare your report for our anthropology class?

Student 2: I'm not sure. I working tonight until 10:00 PM, and tomorrow morning I'm going take my car to the shop for a tune up. When you are going to have time for your work?

Student 1: I'm plan to stay up all night tonight if I have to. I am work all day tomorrow, and I really want to finish the paper before the deadline.

Student 2: Is you going to be online tonight after 10:00 PM? Maybe we can chat and help each other.

Student 1: That sounds like a good idea. I'm going to doing some research online soon, and then I can start to put my ideas together. I'll contact you later tonight.

Student 2: OK. Talk to you then.

Activity 6

Look at the following student's calendar for tomorrow and write four sentences about her plans. Use be going to + *verb in two of your sentences and the present progressive in two sentences. Follow the example.*

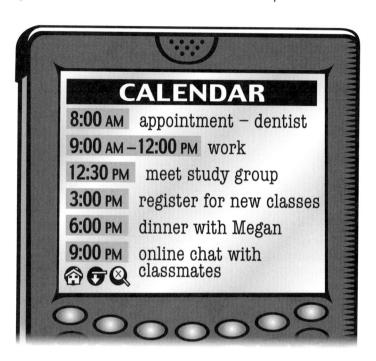

CALENDAR

8:00 AM	appointment – dentist
9:00 AM – 12:00 PM	work
12:30 PM	meet study group
3:00 PM	register for new classes
6:00 PM	dinner with Megan
9:00 PM	online chat with classmates

EXAMPLES: Tomorrow she is going to do some work for school.

OR   Tomorrow she is preparing for her class.

_____

_____

_____

_____

_____

_____

_____

_____

Activity 7

A. Making predictions

1. *What can you predict about your life? Answer the two questions below. In one answer use* will *and in the other answer use* be going to.

   a. What can you say about your life in five years?

      _____

      _____

   b. What can you say about your life ten years from now?

      _____

      _____

2. *On a separate piece of paper, write your sentences from above. Don't tell anyone your predictions, fold your paper, and give it to your teacher. Your teacher will read each person's predictions, and the class will guess who wrote each one.*

B. Making plans

Write at least two sentences about your plans for school or work for the next few months. Include information about your plans for taking online/hybrid classes. You may write negative answers (about things you do not plan to do) as well.

_____

_____

_____

_____

_____

_____

Real If

General Time and Future Time with *If*

[1]Ron likes to take at least one online class every semester. [2]If he **takes** more than one class, the second one **is** usually a hybrid. [3]Right now he is thinking about his future schedule. [4]If he **takes** two online classes next semester, he **will enroll** in two hybrid classes instead of only one.

Presentation

Questions

1. What is the time in sentence 1? How do you know this? What is the time in sentence 2? How do you know this?

2. How many clauses are in sentence 2? What word is putting these clauses together? What form of the verb do you see in each clause?

3. What is the time of sentence 4? How do you know this?

4. How many clauses are in sentence 4? What word is putting these clauses together? What form of the verb do you see in each clause?

Explanation—Using Real *If* in General and Future Time

(Refer to *Destinations 1 Writing for Academic Success*, Unit 5, Part 3, pp. 126–138.)

1. In the Destinations 1 writing book, you learned about using the subordinating conjunction *if* for sentences with a condition and result.

   You learned the following:

   a. As a subordinating conjunction, *if* can join two clauses either at the beginning of a sentence or in the middle.

   b. In either case the sentence has a dependent (subordinate) clause and an independent (main) clause. The clause that begins with *if* is the dependent (subordinate) clause.

c. When the conjunction *if* is in the middle of the sentence, do not add a comma. Add a comma at the end of the first clause when the conjunction *if* is at the beginning of the sentence.

> Students use email, discussion groups, and forums to communicate
> independent clause

> with their classmates *if* they take an online class.
> conjunction   dependent clause

> *If* students take an online class, they use email, discussion groups,
> conjunction   dependent clause   independent clause

> and forums to communicate with their classmates.

2. We often use *if* to express something that is a real possibility both in general time or future time. In each case *if* expresses a condition, and the clause after *if* expresses a possible result.

a. **General time**

> If Ron *takes* more than one online class, the second one *is usually*
> condition   result
> a hybrid.

We know the time in this sentence is general for two reasons: the time word (*usually*) and the verb forms (simple present).

b. **Future**

> If Ron *takes* two online classes *next semester,* he *will enroll* in two
> condition   result
> hybrid classes instead of only one.

We know the time is future in this sentence because of the time expression (*next semester*) and the word *will*. However, we do not use the word *will* in both clauses. We only use *will* in the independent clause. The verb in the dependent clause is a simple present verb form.

> If Ron *takes* two online classes *next semester,* he *is going to enroll* in two hybrid classes instead of only one.

We also use *be going to* in the same way as *will* for future conditions/results. We do not use *be going to* in the dependent clause. The verb in the dependent clause is in simple present form.

Practice

Activity 1   (Review subordinating conjunctions in *Destinations 1 Writing for Academic Success*—Unit 5, pp. 127–138.)

Circle the verbs and any words or expressions that indicate time in the following sentences. If the verb is negative, circle the auxiliary (helping verb) and negative as well. Follow the example.

A. General Time

1. If a student (needs) to feel part of a class, s/he (usually doesn't take) an online class.

2. Students often do well in an online class if they like to prepare assignments on time or before a deadline.

3. If a student likes face-to-face class discussions, usually s/he doesn't enjoy an online class.

4. A student frequently chooses a more traditional class instead of an online one if s/he prefers to have detailed explanations for each assignment.

B. Future

1. If Rob's work schedule changes next semester, he is going to take an online class.

2. Jane will probably get an A in that class if she finishes the final project on time.

3. You will probably feel uncomfortable without face-to-face discussions with your classmates and instructor if you take that history class online.

4. If Jenne feels comfortable with minimal contact with the instructor for explanations, she is going to try a hybrid reading class next semester.

Activity 2

Write G *for general time or* F *for future on the line next to each sentence below. Be prepared to explain your answers.*

_____   1.   If students have very little time to travel and sit in class at school for several hours a week, they sometimes enroll in online classes.

_____   2.   If a student has trouble reading and understanding a college level textbook easily, usually it is not a good idea for this student to sign up for an online class.

_____   3.   Phil will sign up for an online class next year if he doesn't have enough time to commute to school then.

_____   4.   I am going to think about taking an online accounting class if I improve my reading ability by next year.

_____   5.   If a student works independently, she/he usually feels comfortable in an online class.

_____   6.   If a student doesn't know how to use the Internet as a resource for schoolwork, she/he probably doesn't think about taking an online class.

_____   7.   If I read a chapter in my biology text, I usually understand it right away.

_____   8.   If I read the assigned chapter in my grammar book tonight, I'm probably going to call you for help.

Activity 3   (Review subordinating conjunctions in *Destinations 1 Writing for Academic Success*—Unit 5, pp. 127–138.)

A.   **General Time**   *Fill in the spaces with the correct form of the verb in parentheses. Be sure to make the verb negative where indicated.*

1.   If Al (receive) _____ an email from his professor, he

(respond) _____ to it as soon as possible.

2.   If my classmates (get) _____ a homework assignment

in their hybrid class, they all (complete) _____ it

before the deadline.

3.   Usually if we (get) _____ an assignment from

Professor Barbera, we (understand) _____ it.

4.   If I (take) _____ a class at my local college, I usually

(participate–*negative*) _____ in the class discussions.

B. **Future Time**   *Fill in the spaces with the correct form of the verb in parentheses. Be sure to add* will *or* be going to *in the independent clauses.*

1. Right now I do not have Internet access. If I (get)

   _____ a new computer in the next week,

   I (think) _____ about taking an online class.

2. If Jim (receive) _____ your email

   about the class before 5:00 p.m. tonight, he (answer)

   _____ it immediately.

3. Debbie and Bill (work) _____ the new

   assignment tonight if they (receive) _____

   the instructions soon.

4. If Marta (understand–*negative*) _____

   the new assignment from Professor Barbera, she (send)

   _____ an email to him for help.

C. *Fill in the spaces with the correct form of the verb in parentheses. If the time of the sentence is future, be sure to add* will *or* be going to *in the correct space.*

1. If I (send) _____ an email to my instructor

   tonight, I (attach) _____ a file of my work.

2. If I (send) _____ an email to my instructor,

   I often (attach) _____ a file of my work.

3. Glenn always (spend) _____ at least half an

   hour a day in a chat room if he (take) _____

   an online class.

4. If Glenn (participates) _____ in the

   chat room for that class tonight, he (spend)

   _____ at least half an hour there.

5. Betty and Ana (check) _____ email for late

   messages if they (have) _____ time at the

   end of each day.

6. If we (have) _____ time later tonight, we

   (check) _____ our email for late messages.

Activity 4

Find and correct four mistakes in the following chat room discussion.

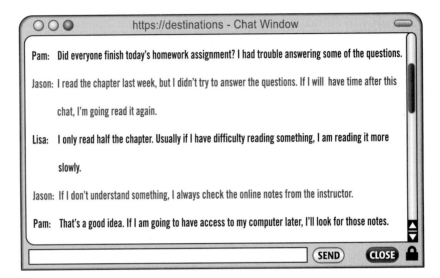

Pam: Did everyone finish today's homework assignment? I had trouble answering some of the questions.

Jason: I read the chapter last week, but I didn't try to answer the questions. If I will have time after this chat, I'm going read it again.

Lisa: I only read half the chapter. Usually if I have difficulty reading something, I am reading it more slowly.

Jason: If I don't understand something, I always check the online notes from the instructor.

Pam: That's a good idea. If I am going to have access to my computer later, I'll look for those notes.

 Activity 5

Combine each pair of sentences using the conjunction if. *Write each sentence out completely and be sure to include correct punctuation. Use pronouns as well. Follow the examples.*

1. Kate feels like an outsider in her class. Kate loses interest in it.

   If Kate feels like an outsider in her class, she loses interest in it.

   Kate will feel like an outsider in her new class tonight. Kate will probably look for another class.

   Kate will probably look for another class if she feels like an outsider in her new class tonight.

2. A student hands in a paper. A student usually expects the teacher to comment on it and return it.

   _____

   A student will hand in a paper later today. The teacher is going to return it by next week.

   _____

3. Sally types an entire research paper. This often takes her several hours to complete it.

   _____

   Sally will type her entire research paper tonight. Sally is going to be up all night working on it.

   _____

4. Usually Pedro needs to download new applications to his computer. Pedro does not get upset about it.

_____

_____

Ariana needs to download a new application to do her work tonight. Ariana is going to be upset.

_____

_____

5. The teacher assigns a group project. Some students get nervous.

_____

The teacher will assign a group project in class this afternoon. We will get together and complete it as soon as possible.

_____

_____

W   *Activity 6*   (Review subordinating conjunctions in *Destinations 1 Writing for Academic Success*—Unit 5, pp. 127–138.)

Complete the following sentences with any information. Be sure to add any necessary punctuation.

1. If I feel uncomfortable in a class _____

_____

2. Usually I _____

   if I type my reports for a class.

3. If I have time later tonight _____

_____

4. Sometimes I _____

   if I think the work is difficult in a class.

5. If I take a hybrid class next semester _____

_____

Gerunds

Gerunds as Subjects and Objects

[1]**Enrolling** in an online class is one way students can continue their education. [2]**Taking** these classes saves travel time and costs for some students. [3]Of course, **paying** attention to certain requirements is important in these courses.

Presentation 1

Questions

1. What is the main verb of each sentence in the caption?

   Sentence 1 _____

   Sentence 2 _____

   Sentence 3 _____

2. What ending do you see on each of the bold words in these sentences? Why do these words have this ending?

Explanation—Gerunds as Subjects

1. A *gerund* is the *-ing* form of a verb. (See Unit 1, Lesson 6 for spelling rules about adding *-ing* to verbs.)

   However, a gerund acts like a noun in a sentence. It is not the verb of that sentence or clause.

   > *Enrolling* in an online class *is* one way students can continue
   >   gerund   verb
   > their education.

   Do not confuse a gerund with a progressive verb in a sentence.

   > *Taking* an online class *is helping* me save travel time and money.
   >   gerund   present progressive verb

2. We often use a gerund as the subject of a sentence. When a gerund is a subject, it is always singular. This means the verb that follows must also be singular.

   > *Taking* an online class *saves* travel time and money for some students.

   > *Paying* attention to certain requirements *is* important in these courses.

3. To make a negative gerund, add the word *not* before the gerund.

   Not preparing for a class is a problem for some students.

   Not paying attention to the requirements can cause problems for some students.

4. We can also use gerunds in questions. Follow the rules for making questions.

   a. *Yes/No questions*

   Put an auxiliary (helping verb) or main verb *be* to the left of the subject (gerund).

   - *Taking* an online class *is* interesting.

subject-gerund   be

     Is taking an online class interesting?*

be subject-gerund

   - *Taking* an online class *saves* travel time.

subject-gerund   verb

     Does taking an online class *save* travel time?**

auxiliary subject-gerund   verb

   - *Taking* an online computer class *can become* fun for some people.

subject-gerund   modal verb

     Can taking an online computer class *become* fun for some people?***

modal subject-gerund   verb

   b. **Question word questions**

   Put the question word and an auxiliary (helping verb) or main verb *be* to the left of the subject.

   > *Why is taking* an online class difficult?

question word be subject-gerund

   > *How does taking* an online class *save* travel time?

question word auxiliary subject-gerund   verb

   > *When can taking* an online computer class *become* fun for people?

question word modal subject-gerund   verb

5. Sometimes a gerund may be by itself before the verb of a sentence and other times there may be other words between the gerund and the verb.

   Studying is fun for some people.

gerund verb

   Studying late at night on a computer *is* easy for some people.

gerund   verb

---

* To review using *be* as a main verb in a sentence, see *Destinations 1 Writing and Grammar,* Unit 2.

** To review making questions with simple present verbs and the auxiliary *do,* see Unit 1, Lesson 5.

*** To review making questions with modals, see Unit 4, Lessons 22–26.

Practice

Activity 1

Underline the gerund and the main verb in each sentence or question below. Follow the example.

1. <u>Having</u> a computer with access to the Internet <u>is</u> necessary for taking an online class.

2. Does learning through computers and the Internet seem difficult to you?

3. Improving skills on the Internet gives students more resources for information.

4. Posting messages and assignments on the Internet is common in an online class.

5. Not participating in online discussions can be a problem.

Activity 2   (Review subordinating conjunctions in *Destinations 1 Writing for Academic Success*—Unit 5, pp. 127–138.)

Write the gerund form of one of the words from the list below in each space. Use each word only one time.

work	offer	enroll	communicate	come

_____ distance education courses is becoming more and more popular at many schools. There are many reasons students may want to take these classes. For example, _____ to class on a regular basis is difficult for some students because they have families to take care of. For other students _____ on a computer feels more comfortable than face-to-face classroom discussions. _____ full time can also make it difficult for some people to come to school. _____ in an online or hybrid class is a good option for many people because it can help them succeed in school.

Activity 3

Change each statement below into a question. Follow the example.

1. Using technology in the classroom can help students understand the material.

   Can using technology in the classroom help students understand the material?

2. Spending time on the Internet for recreation is only one reason for using the Web.

   _____

   _____

3. Buying conveniences such as PDAs gives students a way to be more organized.

   _____

   _____

4. Owning electronic devices often helps people at work and at school.

   _____

   _____

5. Increasing interactive activities in the classroom can make lessons more interesting.

   _____

   _____

[1]Many students of all ages **enjoy using** computers for their schoolwork. [2]They often **appreciate taking** advantage of the information on the Internet.

Presentation 2

Questions

1. What word is the main verb of each sentence in the caption?

   Sentence 1 _____

   Sentence 2 _____

2. What kind of word follows the main verb in each sentence?

Explanation—Gerunds as Objects

1. In Presentation 1 you learned about gerunds, the *-ing* form of a verb acting like a noun in the sentence. You learned that a gerund can be the subject of a sentence. A gerund can also be an object after certain verbs.

    Studying with computers can be fun.
    gerund-subject   verb

    Taking hybrid classes is often convenient.
    gerund-subject   verb

    José enjoys his hybrid class.   José enjoys *studying* for his hybrid class.
    subject verb   object   subject verb   gerund-object

2. Some common verbs followed by a gerund are:

advise	consider	explain	keep (continue)	postpone	risk	think about
appreciate	discuss	feel like	mind (not like)	practice	suggest	understand
avoid	dislike	finish	miss	quit	support	
celebrate	enjoy	imagine	permit	recommend		

    (For a more complete list of these verbs, see Appendix F, page 278.)

3. Gerunds can also follow the verb *go* when someone is discussing certain activities, in particular enjoyable or more recreational activities.

    People often *go surfing* on the web when they are looking for information or games and other activities.

    Yesterday I *went looking* for some new websites to practice my spelling.

Activity 4 (Review transitions in *Destinations 1 Writing for Academic Success*—Unit 4, pp. 98–105.)

Do two things in the following sentences: (a) underline the gerunds acting as objects; (b) circle the gerunds acting as subjects.

1. a. Presenting a lesson through PowerPoint is one technological tool for instructors to use in the classroom.

    b. In addition, some teachers consider using the Internet as another tool in the classroom.

2. a. Completing a full load of classes each semester may be impossible for some students with jobs or family responsibilities.

    b. Therefore, for these students a counselor may advise limiting classes to one or two online or hybrid courses.

3. a. Taking noncredit classes online is part of a broader definition of distance education.

b. For example, some people may avoid registering in semester length classes, but they will take shorter non-credit online classes to fit their schedules.

c. In addition, sometimes supervisors may recommend enrolling in one-day or weekend seminars, so their employees can increase their knowledge and skills for their jobs.

Activity 5   (Review subordinating conjunctions in *Destinations 1 Writing for Academic Success*—Unit 5, pp. 127–138.)

Fill in the spaces with the gerund form of words from the following list. Use each word only one time.

communicate	find	upset	include
bring	participate	attend	see

1. _____ in online chats and discussions

a
   is often necessary in hybrid courses. If you do not mind
   _____ with classmates on a computer,

b
   you might think about _____ one of

c
   these classes in your schedule.

2. If you can't attend classes on campus more than once a week,
   I suggest _____ a hybrid class.

a
   _____ class on campus only once a

b
   week is typical for these kinds of classes.

3. _____ a laptop to a class is acceptable for

a
   some instructors. Other instructors dislike _____

b
   students use these computers during class. Therefore, students should
   not risk _____ their instructors with these

c
   computers in a class.

Activity 6

A. *Find and correct three mistakes in the following sentences.*

Are traveling to a class on campus three times a week a problem for you? If so, some people might suggest to look for a hybrid class. Go to a class on campus only once a week could be the answer to your problem.

B. *Find and correct four mistakes in the following sentences.*

Understanding the requirements of an online course is very important.

1. Use a computer is a very important requirement for this kind of class. No feeling comfortable with email or the Internet makes it very difficult to take this kind of course.

2. Accessing the Internet is necessary for online classes because to complete requirements for an online class often consists of lots of email and online discussions with classmates. Also, know different applications will help students be successful.

Activity 7

Discuss using computers for school or online/hybrid classes in your answers.

A. *Complete the following sentences with a gerund as the subject.*

1. _____ is difficult on a computer.

2. _____ makes some students nervous.

3. _____ takes a lot of time to complete.

4. _____ is easier/more difficult than face-to-face discussions in class.

B. *Complete the following sentences with any information.*

1. Learning a new language on a computer _____

2. Taking online classes _____

3. Using technology in the classroom _____

4. Communicating with classmates in real time on a computer _____

_____

C. *Write four sentences about using computers for school or technology in the classroom. Start two sentences with a gerund using one of the words in the list below. In the other two sentences use one of the words in the list as a verb of the sentence and follow it with a gerund as object. Follow the examples.*

| finish | practice | understand | celebrate | explain | enjoy |

1. *Celebrating the end of a course can be fun with a potluck meal with classmates.*

2. *Sometimes students celebrate finishing a class with a potluck meal with classmates.*

3. _____

4. _____

5. _____

6. _____

Infinitives and Gerunds

Infinitives as Objects/
Verbs with Gerunds and Infinitives

¹Laura **decided to bring** her laptop to school.
²Her teacher **allows students to use** laptops in the classroom, so Laura **hopes to take** notes on hers in class today.

Presentation 1

Questions

1. Look at the bold words in sentence 1. What words follow the verb in this sentence? Look at the bold words in the second clause of sentence 2. What words follow the verb?

2. Look at the bold words in the first clause of sentence 2. How are these different from the other bold words?

Explanation—Infinitives as Objects

1. Infinitives (*to* + simple/base form of the verb) follow certain verbs. We can divide these verbs into three groups.

   a. Use the infinitive form after these verbs.

afford	agree	appear	attempt	can't afford	can't wait
decide	fail	grow	hope	intend	learn
manage	mean	offer	plan	prepare	pretend
refuse	seem	wait			

   (For a more complete list of this group of verbs, see Appendix G, page 278.)

   Laura *decided to bring* her laptop to school. She *hopes to take* notes in her class today.

b. The following verbs require an object (a noun or pronoun) before the infinitive.

advise	allow	cause	convince	encourage	force
get	hire	invite	order	permit	persuade
remind	require	teach	tell	urge	warn

(For a more complete list of this group of verbs, see Appendix H, page 279.)

Laura's teacher *allows students to use* laptops in the classroom.
　　　　　　　　 verb　　　object　　infinitive

Laura's friends *advised her to be* careful with the laptop in the classroom.
　　　　　　　 verb　　object infinitive

c. A few verbs can be followed by an infinitive with or without an object.

ask	choose	expect	help	need	pay
promise	request	want	wish	like	

Jim *needs to get* more information about hybrid classes.

Jim *needs the counselor to give* him more information about hybrid classes.

2. To make a negative infinitive, add the word *not* before the infinitive.

We decided *not to have* an online discussion this afternoon.

The teacher *asked Laura not to bring* her laptop to class again.

Practice

Activity 1　　(Review subordinating conjunctions in *Destinations 1 Writing for Academic Success*—Unit 5, pp. 127–138.)

A. Circle all the verb + infinitive combinations in the following sentences.

1. The instructor agreed to extend the deadline for the new assignment.

2. The instructor prepared to make a PowerPoint presentation because she wanted to show graphs and pictures as part of the lesson.

3. The students seemed not to understand the assignment, so the instructor gave more instructions about it.

4. If students take an online class, they should manage to work independently most of the time.

5. Some students plan to enroll in non-degree classes because they can't afford to spend the time to get a degree.

B.   *Circle all the verb + object + infinitive combinations in the following sentences.*

1.   Sometimes if I am online, my friends invite me to participate in
     a chat room.

2.   The instructor encouraged her students to complete the assignment
     during the remaining class time.

3.   Sometimes if Joan is tired, she has to force herself to complete her
     homework.

4.   Sylvia advised her friends not to miss any face-to-face discussion classes
     for their hybrid class because the instructor is very strict about attendance.

Activity 2   (Review subordinating conjunctions in *Destinations 1 Writing for Academic
Success*—Unit 5, pp. 127–138.)

*Circle the correct letter to complete each sentence. In some cases both answers
may be correct.*

1.   He attempted _____ in the real time discussion because it was
     a class requirement.

     a.   to participate

     b.   his friend to participate

2.   The instructor reminded _____ an online forum at least
     twice a week.

     a.   to join

     b.   her students to join

3.   Ahmad convinced _____ in an online course with him.

     a.   his friends to enroll

     b.   to enroll

4.   The instructor will tell _____ their entire papers electronically
     if they complete them by tonight.

     a.   to send

     b.   the students to send

5.   The instructor promised _____ the rough draft with comments
     before the weekend.

     a.   the class to return

     b.   to return

6. Some students can't wait _____ an online class . . .

   a. to try

   b. them to try

. . . because it allows _____ a flexible schedule.

   a. to have

   b. them to have

7. The instructor expects _____ this unit in the textbook today if the students bring their books.

   a. the students to complete

   b. to complete

Activity 3

A. *Change the order of the words below each line to make good sentences. Write each sentence on the blank line and be sure to add punctuation and capitalization. You do not need to add any other words to your sentences. Follow the example.*

1. _I decided to take an online class this semester._ _____

   decided / an online class / this semester / I / to take

2. _____

   to register / intends / she / tomorrow / for that class

3. _____

   a computer and the Internet / learned / for her hybrid class / to use / Sara

4. _____

   failed / last semester / for that online class / to enroll / in time / they

B. *Do the same as above for A. In these sentences you will also have an object between the verb and the infinitive.*

1. _____

   yesterday / my laptop to school / me / persuaded / my friend / to bring

2. _____

   the class / during class time / warned / for email / the teacher / not to use laptops

3. _____

   require / during class / some instructors / to access the Internet / students

4. _____

   at any time during class / do not permit / other teachers / to use computers / anyone

Presentation 2

Questions

1. Put a line under the main verb of each of the clauses in these sentences. What kind of word follows each of these verbs?

2. Is there any difference in meaning using either the gerund or the infinitive after these verbs?

[1]Lynn **likes to take** online classes sometimes, but she also **likes taking classes** on campus for face-to-face discussions sometimes. [2]Lynn's husband **prefers taking** hybrid classes, but **she prefers not to take** them.

Explanation—Verbs Followed by Either a Gerund or an Infinitive

1. There is a small group of verbs that can be followed by either a gerund or an infinitive. The meaning stays the same when either a gerund or infinitive follows these verbs.

begin	can't stand	continue	hate	like
love	prefer	start	try	

   Lynn *likes to take* online classes, but she also *likes taking classes* on campus sometimes.

2. For a few verbs there is a difference in meaning when you use a gerund or an infinitive.

   a. **stop**

   Joe *stopped taking* hybrid classes because he didn't have time to go to any classes on campus.

   (He took some hybrid classes, but then he stopped. Now he no longer takes them.)

   Joe *stopped to take* a break because he was tired from working on the computer.

   (The reason he stopped was to take a break. He stopped in order to take a break.)

b. **remember**

I *remember registering* for the hybrid class, but now I can't find the information about it.

(I know I registered, and I remember doing that.)

I *remembered to register* for the class before the deadline.

(I registered for the class. I did not forget to register for it.)

c. **forget**

The instructor *forgot to assign* a new chapter to read for the next class.

(She did not remember to give a new reading assignment.)

The instructor *forgot assigning* a project for the next class, so the students were upset about the new reading assignment.

(She forgot that she gave them a project, and then she gave them another assignment. She made the first assignment, but she forgot that she did it.)

Practice

Activity 4   (Review subordinating conjunctions in *Destinations 1 Writing for Academic Success*—Unit 5, pp. 127–138.)

In each sentence change the gerund to an infinitive if it does not change the meaning of the sentence. If this is not possible, write no change. *Follow the example.*

1. I began registering _____to register_____ for a hybrid class on

   my school's website late last night. However, I was already in the class!

   I didn't remember enrolling _____ in it a couple

   of weeks before.

2. Joe stopped attending _____ classes last

   semester because his work hours changed, and he could no longer

   travel to school. If his work schedule continues to change, he will try

   finding _____ an online class next semester.

3. Many students like taking _____ online

a

or hybrid courses because those classes are convenient for

their busy schedules. However, some students prefer signing up

_____ for classes on campus because they

b

like face-to-face discussions.

Activity 5   (Review coordinating conjunctions in *Destinations 1 Writing for Academic*
Success—Unit 3, pp. 66–75 and subordinating conjunctions, Unit 5, pp. 127–138.)

Circle the correct form in parentheses for each sentence. In some cases you will
circle both forms.

Last semester I needed (me to take / to take) one more required course

a

for my major. I started (taking / to take) a hybrid course because my

b

friends urged (me to try / to try) an online class. Unfortunately, I couldn't

c

continue (to attend / attending) because I had family problems. I wanted

d

(to complete / myself to complete) the course, but it was impossible.

e

This semester my friends are telling (to start / me to start) the class

f

again because they are enrolling in it. I love (to have / having) that

g

kind of schedule, so I am going to begin (studying / to study) this

h

course again. This time I refuse (them to give up / to give up) and

i

plan (myself to complete / to complete) the course with my friends.

j

Activity 6   (Review subordinating conjunctions in *Destinations 1 Writing for Academic Success*—Unit 5, pp. 127–138.)

Find one mistake with gerunds or infinitives in each sentence and show how to correct each one.

Tips for success in online classes:

1. At the very beginning learn using the online system for the course, for example, Blackboard or Web CT. You should consider to practice this system's access to the class syllabus, schedules, requirements, and methods of communication. This will you allow to be comfortable with the system right away.

2. You should always avoid to feel alone or isolated in an online class. Students in these courses can't afford stay silent. In other words, they should keep to participate in chats, discussion boards, and forums because they need to become part of the class.

3. If you have a question or problem, you should not pretend understand. This could cause you getting behind in your work and may make more problems for you. You not should wait to ask questions or contact the instructor as soon as possible if you need help.

Activity 7

Write three to five sentences about your opinion of or experiences with online or hybrid classes. Use a different one of the following verbs and a gerund or infinitive in each of your sentences. Follow the example.

agree	consider	decide	dislike	enjoy	explain	help
like	plan	prefer	refuse	require	start	want

EXAMPLE: I don't like online classes because I need to have

discussions with people in class.

_____

_____

_____

_____

_____

_____

_____

_____

_____

Past Progressive (Continuous)*

Past Progressive *vs.* Simple Past

Presentation

¹Yesterday at 1:00 p.m. a storyteller **arrived** and **started** to tell the children some interesting tales. ²At 2:00 p.m. she **was** still **telling** her stories, and the children **were listening** to every word. ³By 2:30 p.m. some of them **were not paying** attention. ⁴**Were** her stories **keeping** all the childrens' interest?

Questions

1. Look at the words in bold in sentence 1. What is the time of this sentence? What ending do you see on these verbs?

2. a. Look at the words in bold in sentence 2. What do you see at the end of each bold verb? What other words in bold do you see with these verbs?

   b. Below are the words in bold from sentence 2. Write the subject of each of these in the spaces next to the words.

   _____ was telling

   _____ were listening

3. Look at the bold words in sentence 3. How are they different from the words in bold in all the other sentences?

4. Look at sentence 4. How do you make a question using these verb forms?

---

*Note: Some books use the word continuous and not progressive. Progressive and continuous have the same meaning.

Explanation—Past Progressive (Continuous)

1. a. In Unit One, Lesson 2 you learned about the simple past. Simple past verbs tell us that something happened one time and finished in the past.

    Yesterday at 1:00 p.m. a storyteller *arrived* and *started* to tell her tales.

    b. You also learned about present progressive (continuous) verbs in Unit One (Lessons 6 and 7). Present progressive includes two words: the present of the auxiliary (helping verb) *be* and the verb with an *-ing* ending. These verb forms tell us that at the present time something is continuing or in progress/not finished.

    The children *are listening* to the storyteller *right now.*

2. We can also use progressive verbs in the past. These verb forms also include two words, but in this case the auxiliary (helping verb) *be* is in the past.

    past of auxiliary (helping verb) *be (was/were)* + verb + *-ing**
                                    1   2   3

    At 2:00 p.m. she *was telling* stories to the children.
                      1   2 3

    The children *were listening* to every word.
                  1   2   3

    Be sure to have all three pieces for these verb forms.

3. Use these verb forms for past actions that were in progress or continuous at a certain time in the past. The actions started before that specific time, were in progress at that time, and perhaps continued beyond that time.

    At 2:00 p.m. all the children *were paying* attention to the stories.

    Were the children finished paying attention at 2:00 p.m., or were they continuing to pay attention?

4. Do not use these forms for non-action (stative) verbs. (See Unit 1, Lesson 8.) Do not use these forms for one-time completed actions in the past.

    The children *seemed* very interested in the stories for the entire time.

    At 1:00 p.m. the storyteller *arrived.* The children saw her enter the room.

5. **Negative sentences**

    Follow the rule for making a sentence negative.

    RULE: Add the word *not* after the auxiliary (helping verb) *be* to make a sentence negative.

    Some of the children *were not (weren't**) paying* attention to all the stories.

    The storyteller *was not (wasn't**) telling* stories all night long.

---

*See Unit One, Lesson 6, page 36 for spelling changes with *-ing.*
**Contractions are often used in conversation. They are not usually used in formal writing.

Follow this pattern for negative sentences using past progressive verbs:

subject	auxiliary (be) (helping verb)	not	verb + -ing	
Some of the children	were	not	paying	attention to all the stories.
The storyteller	was	not	telling	stories all night long.

6. **Questions**

   a. *Yes/No* **questions**

   Follow the rule for making a question: Move the auxiliary (helping verb) *be* to the left of the subject.

   Was the storyteller *talking* all night long?

   Were her stories *keeping* all the children's interest?

Follow this pattern for *yes/no* questions with past progressive verbs:

auxiliary (be) (helping verb)	subject	verb + -ing	
Was	the storyteller	talking	all night long?
Were	her stories	keeping	all the students' interest?

   b. **Question word questions**

   Follow the rule for making a question: Add the question word and move the auxiliary (helping verb) *be* to the left of the subject.

   When was the storyteller *talking* to the students?

   Why were the students *listening* to all the stories?

Follow this pattern for question word questions with past progressive verbs:

question word	auxiliary (be) (helping verb)	subject	verb + -ing	
When	was	the storyteller	talking	to the students?
Why	were	the students	listening	to all the stories?
Where	was	the storyteller	speaking	to the children?
What	were	the children	doing	last night?
Who	was**	*	listening	to all the stories?

*NOTE: Do not include a subject in these questions because the answer to *Who* is the subject.
**Always use the auxiliary (helping verb) *was* in these questions.

Practice

Activity 1

Circle both the auxiliary (helping verb) and the verb for all the past progressive verb forms in the following paragraph.

Yesterday the storyteller was talking to the children for two hours. During that time the children seemed happy to listen because she was telling them thrilling legends and tales. In some of these stories she was exaggerating the abilities of the heroes. At the end of her storytelling, the children were asking many questions for quite a while. Most of them were listening carefully to all of her answers.

Activity 2

A. *Fill in each space with the past progressive form of one of the verbs on the list below. Use each verb only one time.*

talk	complete	discuss	think	read

1. After class yesterday some of my friends _____ their favorite Greek myths at the library all afternoon.

2. Bob _____ to his sister about Norse myths for a long time yesterday afternoon.

3. After dinner last night I _____ about people from long ago and their need to tell these kinds of stories.

4. Late last night a few people _____ many different tales and legends in a chat room on the Internet.

5. At the same time some other friends _____ an assignment for school about different versions of the creation of the world.

B. *Change each sentence above into a negative sentence.*

1. _____

    _____

2. _____

_____

3. _____

_____

4. _____

_____

5. _____

_____

Activity 3

Find and correct one mistake in each of the following sentences.

1. For many years, ancient people were create stories to explain the origins of the world and the people in it.

2. They were useing an oral tradition to tell these myths and legends.

3. In other words, they passing these stories from generation to generation through storytelling.

4. Did these myths and legends remaining exactly the same through all the years of storytelling?

5. People were making changes through the years, so some people were hearing different versions.

6. Probably for many years people were believing these stories as facts.

Activity 4

Look back at the paragraph in Activity 1 and read it again. Then write questions about this paragraph to fit the answers given below. Your first two questions should be yes/no questions, and the next three questions should use the question word given in parentheses.

Yes/No questions:

1. _____?

Yes, she spoke to them for all that time.

2. _____?

Yes, she was telling them the heroes were like supermen.

Question word questions:

3. (when) _____ ?

   She was telling the children her stories yesterday.

4. (why) _____ ?

   She was thrilling them with her stories.

5. (what) _____ ?

   They were asking many questions at the end of her storytelling session.

Activity 5

Fill in the spaces of the following conversation with the verb in parentheses. Use either simple past or past progressive verb forms in your answers. In some cases both forms might be possible, but you should use past progressive in those cases. Be sure to make your answer negative or a question if indicated.

Charlie: I (try) _____ to call you last night at about 8:00
          p.m., but you (answer–*negative*) _____ your
          phone.

Sherry: Really? I (be) _____ home at that time.

Charlie: Well, what (you-do) _____ ?

Sherry: Maybe I (listen) _____ to one of my books on tape
          at that time. I (go) _____ to the library yesterday,
          and I (look) _____ for some books about Greek
          myths for over an hour. Finally, I (find) _____ a
          tape of some.

Charlie: I (want) _____ to look for some books with stories
          too yesterday, but I (work) _____ all afternoon and
          evening. I (have–*negative*) _____ any time to go to
          the library. Can I borrow your tape?

Sherry: Sure. I'll let you know when I finish with it.

Activity 6

Look at the picture of two people from a special dinner last evening. Write three sentences about what these people were doing and three sentences about what they were not doing in the picture. Use a different verb from the list below in the past progressive form for each sentence.

VERBS:	talk	eat	stand
	discuss	relax	swim
	plan	listen	argue
	enjoy	sleep	

_____

_____

_____

_____

_____

_____

_____

_____

_____

_____

_____

_____

Past Progressive (Continuous)

With Time Clauses and Subordinating Conjunctions of Time

Presentation

[1]Last night Roberto **was telling** stories to his son about his survival in a remote mountain area. [2]While Roberto **was talking**, his son **was listening** carefully. [3]When Roberto **was explaining** one strange occurrence, his son **showed** his surprise. [4]As Roberto **was telling** him another story, his son **started** to ask some questions.

Questions

1. How many clauses are in sentence 1? What is the verb form of the bold words in this sentence?

2. a. How many clauses are in sentence 3? What word is putting these clauses together? Are the verb forms the same in these clauses?

   b. How many clauses are in sentence 4? What word is putting them together? Are the verb forms the same in these clauses?

   c. How many clauses are in sentence 2? What word is putting them together? Are the verb forms the same in these clauses?

3. Which actions in these sentences happened or finished quickly and which ones took a longer time?

Explanation—Past Progressive with Subordinating Conjunctions of Time *(When/While/As)*

1. In Unit Six of the *Destinations 1* writing book, you learned about time clauses with several subordinating conjunctions. (See *Destinations 1 Writing for Academic Success*—Unit 6, Part 3, pp. 155–166.)

   We often use past progressive verb forms with time clauses that begin with three of these conjunctions: *when, while,* and *as.* These conjunctions join an independent and dependent clause and follow the rules about commas and punctuation that you learned in Destinations 1.

2. Sometimes in these cases, one clause uses the simple past and the other clause uses past progressive. In these sentences, the simple past indicates the action is short or finished, but the action in past progressive is longer or in progress/not finished.

   When Roberto *was explaining* one strange occurrence, his son *showed*
                  in progress/not finished   short action
   his surprise.

3. In some cases, the action in past progressive is not finished when the other action takes place. In other words, the action in one clause (simple past) comes in the middle of or interrupts the action in progress in the other clause (past progressive).

   As Roberto *was telling* him another story, his son *started* to ask
              in progress/not finished   interruption
   some questions.

4. In other cases, both clauses use the past progressive because both actions were continuous or in progress at the same time.

   While Roberto *was talking,* his son *was listening* carefully.
           in progress   in progress

5. Sometimes we use the conjunction *when* to show that one action followed very quickly after another. In these cases we use a simple past verb in both clauses.

   Roberto's son *asked* some questions when he *heard* the thrilling story.
   (He heard the story and immediately asked some questions.)

   He *laughed* when he *heard* the humorous story.
   (He heard the story and immediately laughed.)

Practice

Activity 1

A. *Circle the past progressive verb forms as well as the subordinating conjunctions of time.*

1. When people told myths and legends, groups of people were listening to these oral stories.

2. While some people in one culture were explaining a creation story, someone in another culture was giving a different version of creation.

3. Probably some people showed a lot of interest as the storytellers were speaking.

4. Maybe some other people were getting scared when they heard the thrilling stories.

5. As legends were circulating among the people, some storytellers made changes to them.

B. *In the space next to each number, label each of the following sentences with one of the following meanings:*

   S = These two events were happening at the same time.

   I = One event came in the middle of the other (interrupted).

   F = One event immediately followed the other.

_____ 1. When storytellers made changes to legends, some people became more interested in the heroes and their actions.

_____ 2. Sometimes as one person was telling the stories, another person started to write them down.

_____ 3. Other times while one person was telling stories to a group, another person was writing them down.

_____ 4. Last night as the storyteller was making some changes to the story, some people laughed at the humorous part.

_____ 5. When the storyteller made some changes to the story, some people laughed at the humorous part.

_____ 6. The people were laughing while the storyteller was making the story more humorous.

Activity 2   (All the following sentences relate to the story "Pandora's Box" in *Destinations 1 Writing for Academic Success*, page 159.)

Fill in each blank space with the past progressive form of the verb in parentheses. Make your answer negative where indicated.

1. As Jupiter (send) _____ Pandora to Earth, he gave her a box to bring with her.

2. When Jupiter gave Pandora the box, she (think–*negative*) _____ about it.

3. While Jupiter (give) _____ her the box, she (pay) _____ attention to his explanation about it.

4. When Pandora (knock) _____ on Prometheus' door, he (listen–*negative*) _____ to it.

5. Pandora became bored while she (live) _____ with her husband, Epimetheus.

6. When Pandora (look) _____ at the box from Jupiter, she remembered his words to her.

7. As Pandora (took) _____ the lid off the box, devils and demons (fly) _____ out.

8. When all the devils and demons (come) _____ out of the box, Pandora (try) _____ to close the box.

9. As Pandora (look) _____ into the box, she saw one thing left inside, hope.

Activity 3   (Review subordinating conjunctions of time in *Destinations 1 Writing for Academic Success*—Unit 6, pp. 155–166.)

Find one mistake in each sentence and show how to correct each one. The mistakes will be with the verb forms or with the sentence structure (such as fragments).

1. Many people was paying attention to the great storyteller Homer as he was telling stories such as the Odyssey.

2. When Aesop told his fables. He was also giving advice about life through the morals of his stories.

3. We were understanding the exaggeration of the tall tale characters when we were listening to the stories about Paul Bunyan and Pecos Bill.

4. While I listening to the fables by La Fontaine, the animals started to seem more and more human.

5. As the teacher was read the fables to the children, she gave the animals human voices.

6. While the children were listening to Aesop's fables. They were also learning lessons about people and their behavior.

7. Some of the children were believing the teacher's fictitious story as she was reading it.

8. When I was listening to the story, I were thinking about its resemblance to other stories about the same subject.

9. A friend called me on the phone while I read the Odyssey in my room.

Activity 4

Below is a short story about Anansi from the African spider tales. Fill in each blank space with either a simple past form or past progressive form of the verb in parentheses. In some cases both answers may be correct, but you should use the past progressive form as much as possible. Be prepared to explain your answers.

Part A

Anansi (be) _____ clever but not wise, so he
                        1
wanted more wisdom. He (decide) _____ to ask
                                     2
the people in his village to give some of their wisdom to him. As he

(visit) _____ his different neighbors, he (collect)
              3
_____ their wisdom in a hollow gourd. When Anansi
        4
collected enough wisdom, he (make) _____ a plan to
                                          5
hide this gourd at the top of a tree.

Part B

First, he (find) _____ a cloth band. When he
                       1
(tie) _____ the gourd around his waist with this cloth
          2
band, he (put) _____ the gourd on the front of his body.
                      3
As he (climb) _____ up the tree, the gourd (get)
                     4

_____ in his way. He could not make any progress.
                    5

While he (do) _____ this, his youngest son (see)
                                6

_____ him. Then his son (give) _____
              7   8

Anansi a suggestion to put the gourd on his back instead of on his belly.

Part C

When Anansi (reach) _____ the top of the tree, he
                                    1

(realize) _____ his son's wisdom. While Anansi
                  2

(think) _____ about his son's advice, he (get)
                  3

_____ upset about his own wisdom. Therefore, at
              4

the top of the tree, he (open) _____ the gourd and
                                                5

(spill) _____ all the wisdom into the wind. When the
                6

wisdom (blow) _____ out of the gourd, the wind
                            7

(take) _____ it to all parts of the world. This is how the
                8

world (gain) _____ wisdom.
                        9

W   **Activity 5**   (The following sentences are related to the fable "The Milkmaid and Her Pail" in *Destinations 1 Writing for Academic Success*, page 162.)

Complete each sentence with a clause using either simple past or past progressive verb forms. Be sure to use correct punctuation as well. You may want to look back at the story before you write your answers.

1. As the milkmaid was carrying the milk on her head _____

    _____.

2. She _____ while she was walking on the road to market.

3. While she was imagining all the good things about her future _____

    _____.

4. When she was tossing her head _____

    _____.

5. She _____
    as the pail was falling off her head.

6. She _____
    when she was telling her mother the story.

Present Perfect

Indefinite Time *vs.* Simple Past

¹Amy **has read** Aesop's fables many times. ²However, she **has not read** many fables by La Fontaine. ³Some of her friends **have listened** to those stories, and they **have enjoyed** them. ⁴**Have** you **read** any fables?

Presentation

Questions

1. Below are the bold words in sentence 1 and sentence 3. Write the subject that goes with each of them in the space provided.

   _____ has read

   _____ have listened

   _____ have enjoyed

2. What is the time in sentences 1 and 3? Do you think the actions are finished or not finished in these sentences?

3. Look at sentence 2. How do you form the negative with these verb forms?

4. Look at sentence 4. How do you form a *yes/no* question with these verb forms?

Explanation—Present Perfect: Indefinite Past

1. As you learned in Unit One, some verb forms tell us about an event at a specific time, such as simple past or present progressive (now). Often these verb forms work with time words to tell us the time.

   Homer *told* stories *many years ago.* (simple past—many years ago)

   My friends *are listening* to stories by Homer *right now.* (present progressive—now)

2. In other cases we may not use verbs with any specific time. This is one way that we use *present perfect* verbs.

   > Some of Amy's friends *have listened* to stories, and they *have enjoyed* them.

   Amy's friends listened to stories and enjoyed them at some time in the past, but we do not know anything about the specific time.

3. Present perfect verb forms require two words: the auxiliary *has* or *have* and the past participle of a verb.

   a. We use the auxiliary (helping verb) *has* for third person singular subjects (John/he/she/it, etc.). We use *have* for all other subjects.

      > *Amy has* read some fables. *Her friends have* listened to these stories.

   b. What is the past participle of a verb? For regular verbs, we add *-ed*, just as we do for simple past verbs. (See Unit One, Lesson 2 for spelling rules about adding *-ed* to verbs.)

      > Amy's friends *have listened* to these stories, and they *have enjoyed* them.

   c. You must memorize past participles for irregular verbs. (See Appendix A, page 273 for the irregular verb list.)

      > Amy *has read* many fables. Her friends *have heard* some of them.

4. **Negative sentences**

   Follow the rule for making a sentence negative.

   RULE: Add the word *not* after the auxiliary (helping verb) to make a sentence negative.

   > Amy *has not (hasn't)* * *read* many stories by La Fontaine.

   > Her friends *have not (haven't)* * *listened* to many Aesop's fables.

   Follow this pattern for negative sentences with present perfect verb forms:

subject	auxiliary *(have)* (helping verb)	not	verb (past participle)	
Amy	has	not	read	many stories by La Fontaine.
Her friends	have	not	listened	to many Aesop's fables.

5. **Questions**

   a. *Yes/No questions*

      RULE: Place the auxiliary (helping verb) *have* to the left of the subject of the sentence.

      > *Have* you *listened* to any fables? *Has* Amy *read* many Aesop's fables?

   ---

   *Contractions are often used in conversation. They are not usually used in formal writing.

Follow this pattern for yes/no questions with present perfect verb forms:

auxiliary *(have)* (helping verb)	subject	verb (past participle)	
Have	you	listened	to any fables?
Has	Amy	read	many Aesop's fables?

b. **Question word questions**

Place the question word and the auxiliary (helping verb) to the left of the subject.

Why has Amy *read* so many fables?

Where have her friends *listened* to stories by La Fontaine?

Follow this pattern for question word questions with present perfect verb forms:

question word	auxiliary (helping verb)	subject	verb (past participle)	
Why	has	Amy	read	so many fables?
Where	have	her friends	listened	to stories by La Fontaine?
Who	has**	*	listened	to stories by Aesop?

*NOTE: Do not include a subject in these questions because the answer to *Who* is the subject.
**Always use the auxiliary (helping verb) *has* in these questions.

6. Use present perfect verb forms for the following:

a. Events that took place (and finished) at an unspecified time in the past
   In this case we do not know the time, or the time is not important.
   DO NOT use specific time words (such as *last week* or *yesterday*)
   with these verb forms.

   Correct: Amy's friends *have listened* to La Fontaine's fables,
                  and they *have enjoyed* them.

   Incorrect: Amy's friends have listened to fables *yesterday*.
                  They have enjoyed them *last week*.

b. Events that took place more than once in the past (repeated events)
   but there is no specific time.

   We *have listened to* Aesop's fables many times.

   Amy *has read* that book of fables three times.

7. When we use present perfect in this way, the action in the indefinite past has a relationship or connection with the present. The action or event happened and finished in the past, but it often continues to affect the present in some way. In other words, it may have some importance to the present. Therefore, we use these forms for actions of living people only.

> Those storytellers *have visited* my school several times. (They might visit again.)

> Brad Pitt *has performed* in movies about legends, such as Homer's story of Troy. (He may continue to perform in other films.)

REMEMBER: We do not use these forms to discuss actions of people who are no longer living. We discuss their actions with simple past verb forms.

> Aesop *told* many fables. Aesop *was* a famous storyteller.

> (He is not related to the present. He cannot tell stories again now or in the future.)

> NOT: Aesop *has told* many fables. He *has been* a famous storyteller.

Practice

Activity 1

A. *Put a line under all of the present perfect verb forms in the following sentences. Be sure to underline both the auxiliary (helping verb) and the verb as well as any negatives.*

B. *Write the simple form of each underlined verb above its past participle. Follow the example.*

assign
An instructor has assigned her students to write a fable or legend for

homework. She has given them two nights to complete this assignment.

However, some students have experienced difficulty getting started on their

writing assignments for this class. They have not been successful in writing

new stories in short periods of time. Therefore, a few students have asked

for some help and a later deadline. The instructor has thought about these

requests, but she has not made a decision about them. She is probably

going to discuss this more in class later today.

Activity 2

A. *Fill in the spaces with the present perfect form of the verbs in parentheses. Be sure to make your answer negative if indicated. Make spelling changes as necessary.*

1. An English instructor (announce) _____ a contest for writing fables to her class.

2. Several students (enter) _____ writing contests in their other English classes, but they (succeed–*negative*) _____ in winning anything.

3. Joan (complete) _____ two different fables for this contest.

4. Some of her friends (help) _____ her revise these stories.

5. She (start) _____ to write another one as well.

6. She (hand in–*negative*) _____ any of the stories to the teacher.

B. *Fill in the spaces with the present perfect form of the verbs in parentheses. Most of these verbs are irregular. Be sure to make your answer negative if indicated.*

1. Two of Joan's friends also (write) _____ fables for the contest, but they (be–*negative*) _____ happy with their work.

2. Greg (have) _____ trouble getting enough time to write, so he (make–*negative*) _____ enough progress with his stories.

3. Alice (find) _____ it difficult to create a fable with a good moral.

4. They both (spend) _____ hours discussing their work with other people.

5. Each one (try) _____ to write different versions of their stories several times.

Activity 3

A. *Look back at Activity 2 and change the sentences from Part A as indicated below in two ways:*

a. On line *a* make the sentence negative.

b. On line *b* make the sentence a *yes/no* question.

Follow the example:

1. a. An English instructor has not announced a contest for writing fables to her class.

    b. Has an English instructor announced a contest for writing fables in her class?

2. (Change the first clause only.)

    a. _____

    b. _____

3. a. _____

    b. _____

4. a. _____

    b. _____

5. a. _____

    b. _____

B. *Using the words below each line, write question word questions. Do not add or remove any words.*

1. _____

    has / to her class / what / announced / one teacher

2. _____

    of Joan's friends / fables / have / how many / for the contest / written

3. _____

    for the contest / helped / who / Joan / to revise / has / her stories

4. _____

    Greg / had / to write / why / getting enough time / has / trouble

Activity 4

Find and correct nine mistakes in the following paragraph.

Steve and Bill has become upset about their writing. They both have start and stopped writing their stories twice. Yesterday Bill has talked to his instructor for help, and last night he has made more changes to his work. He is saved the newest version on his computer, and he plans to finish the story soon. Steve has tryed to write another story, but he not has been able to complete it. Probably he have experienced *writer's block* with these stories. What he has done to help himself with this problem?

inability
to write

Activity 5

Fill in the spaces with simple past or present perfect verb forms of the verbs in parentheses. In some cases either form may be correct, but you should use present perfect as much as possible. Do not use any other verb forms.

A. (Be) _____ Aesop a real person or a fictitious storyteller?
     1

Some people (say) _____ that he (be) _____
                        2   3

not a real person because we know so little about him. However,

some ancient Greek writers (write) _____ about him
                                    4

in their works. Many people (argue) _____ that he
                                     5

(be) _____ a slave in Greece over two thousand
       6

years ago. Other people (thought) _____
                                   7

that he (live) _____ as a slave and then
               8

(become) _____ free.
          9

B. Some people also (guess) _____ that his origins were
                            1

not Greek, especially because the characters in his stories are usually

animals from Africa and not Greece or Europe. In addition, one scholar

(suggest) _____ that Aesop's name came from an ancient
           2

Greek word for dark-skinned African people or a person of African

descent. Maybe his stories (be) _____ originally folktales
                                3

from an anonymous author, and Aesop (become) _____
                                               4

the storyteller. In any case, his stories (survive) _____ for
                                                    5

everyone to enjoy even today.

Activity 6

Clara and Dennis have writer's block, *so each one has a list of things to do to help with this problem. They each have completed and checked off several items on their lists. There are also uncompleted things on the lists without checks. Write sentences about both the completed and uncompleted tasks on these lists as follows:*

 a. Write two sentences about tasks Clara has completed.

 b. Write two sentences about tasks Dennis has not completed.

 c. Write two sentences about tasks both Dennis and Clara have completed.

 d. Write two sentences about tasks both Dennis and Clara have not completed.

Be sure to use different information in each of your sentences. Follow the examples on page 251.

Dennis' list:

  Remain positive
 ✔ Brainstorm ideas with friends
  and family
  Go to the instructor during office
  hours
 ✔ Take breaks while writing
  Try to relax
  Post to a discussion group online
  Revise drafts several times
  Be flexible to change ideas
  Send an email to the instructor

Clara's list:

 ✔ Visit the library to read fables
  Try to write in different places
 ✔ Do some freewriting exercises
 ✔ Brainstorm ideas with friends
  and family
  Follow a routine to write every day
  at the same time
 ✔ Take breaks while writing
  Try to relax
 ✔ Revise drafts several times
  Send an email to the instructor

EXAMPLES: Clara has revised drafts several times.

Dennis has not revised drafts several times.

a. _____

_____

a. _____

_____

b. _____

_____

b. _____

_____

c. _____

_____

c. _____

_____

d. _____

_____

d. _____

_____

Present Perfect

From Past to Present with *For* and *Since*

Presentation

Questions

1. What is the time in sentence 1? How do you know this?

2. What form of the verb do you see in bold in sentences 2 and 3?

3. What is the time in sentences 2 and 3? What words give information about time in those sentences?

(620-560 BCE)	300 BCE		Today

¹After Aesop's death, other people started to write his stories. ²People **have written** these stories in many languages **since about 300 BCE.** ³In other words, these stories **have been** available for people to read **for over two thousand years.**

Explanation—Present Perfect with *For* and *Since*

1. In Lesson 34 you learned about using present perfect for events or states that took place at an unspecified time or more than one time in the past.

    Sometimes present perfect forms give information about events or states that started in the past, continue to the present, and may even continue into the future.

2. As discussed in Lesson 34, present perfect verb forms require two parts: the auxiliary *have* or *has* (depending on the subject of the sentence) and the past participle of the verb.

3. You will sometimes find present perfect verbs with the words *for* and *since*. Both these words indicate that something started in the past and continues until now as follows:

    *   for = amount of time (how long/duration)

        These stories *have been* available for people to read *for over two thousand years.*
        how long/amount of time

        We *have studied* present perfect verb forms *for one week.*
        how long/amount of time

    *   since = starting time (when this action or state started)

        These stories *have been* available for people to read *since about 300* BC.
        starting time

        We *have studied* present perfect verb forms *since last week.*
        starting time

4. Using *since* with present perfect—conjunction or preposition

    a. Sometimes we use since as a subordinating conjunction. (See *Destinations 1 Writing for Academic Success,* Unit 6, Part 3 for a review of subordinating conjunctions.)

        In these cases, the information after the word *since* will be a dependent clause (subject + verb), and the verb in that clause will be simple past. This is because the information after the word *since* tells us the time the event or state started in the past. However, the information in the independent clause will have a present perfect verb form because that event or state started in the past and continues until now.

        People *have written* collections of Aesop's fables *since he died.*
        present perfect   simple past
        independent clause   dependent clause

        Since we started this unit, we *have read* interesting fables and stories.
        simple past   present perfect
        dependent clause   independent clause

    b. In other cases *since* is a preposition. The words that follow do not make a complete sentence/clause.

        People *have written* collections of Aesop's fables *since his death.*
        preposition—noun

        We *have read* interesting fables *since last week.*
        preposition—noun

5. **Negative sentences**

    Follow the rule for making a sentence negative. (See Lesson 34 for a review of this.)

    These stories *have not (haven't) been* available for over two thousand years.

    We *have not (haven't) studied* present perfect verb forms since last week.

6. **Questions**

Follow the rule for making questions. (See Lesson 34 for a review of this.)

Have many people *written* Aesop's stories since 300 BCE?

How long have these stories *been* available to read?

Practice

Activity 1   (Review subordinating conjunctions of time in *Destinations 1 Writing for Academic Success*—Unit 6, pp. 155–166.)

A. *Circle all the present perfect verb forms.*

B. *Underline the words* for *and* since *as well as the words that follow them. Label* since *as a conjunction with a* C *or as a preposition with a* P.

Jean de La Fontaine lived in the 17th century. He wrote stories until he died in 1695. His stories have survived for several centuries. People have read his fables in many different languages since storytellers translated them from the original French. I have been interested in them for several years. Our class studied some of his stories last semester, but I haven't had time to read more since then. Have you taken a look at any of them since our class ended?

Activity 2   (Review subordinating conjunctions of time in *Destinations 1 Writing for Academic Success*—Unit 6, pp. 155–166.)

A. *Fill in the spaces with the present perfect form of the verbs in parentheses. Then circle the word* (for or since) *that fits the sentence.*

Some of my children's favorite books are collections of myths, legends, and folk tales.

1. These books (belong) _____ to our family (for / since) over 35 years.

2. I (own) _____ one book (for / since) I was a child.

3. My children (hear) _____ these stories (for / since) their childhood, and they still enjoy them.

4. The people in my family (spend) _____ many nights discussing these stories (for / since) many years.

B. *Fill in the spaces with the present perfect form of the verb in parentheses. Then add information after both* for *and* since *that fits the sentence. Follow the example.*

1. I (live) _____ have lived _____ in this city since _____ last year _____ .

                                          for _____ two years _____ .

2. My favorite book (be) _____ Aesop's Fables

     since _____ .

        for _____ .

3. I (listen) _____ to folk tales in my language

     since _____ .

        for _____ .

4. I (read) _____ stories in English since _____ .

                                  for _____ .

5. In this class we (study) _____ the stories in Unit Six

     since _____ .

        for _____ .

C. *Share your answers with a partner. Write your partner's answers to questions 2, 3, and 4 below. Follow the examples.*

1. S/He/my partner has lived in this city since last year.

    S/He/my partner has lived in this city for two years.

2. _____

    _____

3. _____

    _____

4. _____

    _____

Activity 3

Look at the timeline below about dates for stories in Unit Six of Destinations 1 Writing for Academic Success. *First, fill in the blank spaces with the simple past or present perfect of the verbs in parentheses. Then complete the sentence on the blank line with either* for *or* since *followed by information from the timeline. Follow the example.*

Aesop	Scheherazade	La Fontaine	slaves' tales	tall tales	
(620-560 BCE)	800 CE	1600	1700	1800	Today

1. Aesop (write) _____ *wrote* _____ his stories in the 6th century BCE.

   People (heard) _____ *have heard* _____ his stories

   for / (since) _____ *the 6th century BCE.* _____ **OR**

   (for) / since _____ *thousands of years.* _____

2. Aesop (tell) _____ his stories more than two thousand

   years ago. Storytellers (continue) _____ to tell his stories

   for / since _____.

3. Stories about Scheherazade (start) _____ around 800 CE.

   People (circulate) _____ these stories for / since

   _____.

4. La Fontaine (tell) _____ his fables in the 1600s. People

   (listen to) _____ these fables for / since

   _____.

5. African slaves (bring) _____ African spider tales

   to the United States during the 18th century. For / Since

   _____ people (remember) _____

   these stories.

6. *Pioneers* (create) _____ tall tales during their travels in the

   1800s. Their stories (stay) _____ with us for / since

   _____.

people who
moved west

Activity 4   (Review subordinating conjunctions of time in *Destinations 1 Writing for Academic Success*—Unit 6, pp. 155–166.)

Find seven mistakes in the following conversation and correct them.

Steve: What have you talk about in our literature class since I started my absences? Have I missed a lot of work for then?

Diane: Since about a week, we has discussed several new folk tales, including the tall tales of Paul Bunyan and Pecos Bill.

Steve: You've done all of that for last Friday?

Diane: Well this instructor covers quite a bit of material during each class. That's why have try not to be absent at all since the class has started.

Steve: I can see your point. I'll try not to be absent anymore too.

Activity 5   (Review subordinating conjunctions of time in *Destinations 1 Writing for Academic Success*—Unit 6, pp. 155–166.)

A.   *Answer the following questions* yes or no. *If your answer is* no, *go to the next question. If your answer is* yes, *on the line, write how long this has been true for you. Then write a sentence explaining how long this has been true using* for *or* since. *Follow the example.*

1.   Are you able to speak English with native speakers?

☑ yes   ☐ no   how long? _____one year_____

I have been able to speak English with native speakers for one year.

OR

I have been able to speak English with native speakers since last year.

OR

I have been able to speak English with native speakers since I arrived in this country.

2.   Are you a full-time student?

☐ yes   ☐ no   how long? _____

_____

Are you a part-time student?

☐ yes   ☐ no   how long? _____

_____

3. Do you know any famous stories from your culture or in your native language?

❑ yes   ❑ no   how long? _____

_____

Do you know any famous stories from another culture or language?

❑ yes   ❑ no   how long? _____

_____

4. Do you own books of stories or folk tales in your language?

❑ yes   ❑ no   how long? _____

_____

Do you own books of stories or folk tales in English?

❑ yes   ❑ no   how long? _____

_____

B. *Discuss your answers with a partner or in a small group. Write sentences about your classmates' answers.*

_____

_____

_____

_____

_____

_____

_____

Present Perfect with Adverbs

Never/Ever/Yet/Already

¹Some students **have never heard** folk tales or legends in English. ²One student **has already read** some tall tales about Pecos Bill. ³**Have you ever studied** these stories in your classes? ⁴**Have you learned** about Pecos Bill or Paul Bunyan **yet**?

Presentation

Questions

1. What form of the verbs do you see in bold in sentences 1 and 2? Circle the other words in bold with these verbs.

2. In what kind of sentences do you find the words *ever* and *yet* in bold?

3. What is the time in each of these four sentences?

Explanation—Present Perfect with *Never/Ever/Yet/Already*

We often use the following adverbs with present perfect verb forms.

1. **Already**

   One student *has already read* some tall tales about Pecos Bill.

   a. **Meaning:** some time in the past—no specific time

   We know one student read some tall tales, but we do not know exactly when s/he did this. Also, there may be a connection to the present when we use the adverb *already.* The action or state may have some importance to the present. For example, because this student has already read some stories, maybe s/he does not want to read them again now.

   b. **Position in sentence:** usually between the auxiliary (helping verb) *have/has* and the verb

   One student *has already read* some tall tales about Pecos Bill.

   Sometimes you may see *already* at the end of a sentence as well.

   One student *has read* some tall tales about Pecos Bill *already.*

c. **Negative statements:** We do not usually make negative statements with *already* and present perfect verbs.

d. **Questions:** Follow the same rules for making questions with present perfect verbs.

> *Has she already read* some tall tales? *Has she read* some tall tales *already*?

2. **Never**

Some students *have never heard* folk tales or legends in English.

a. **Meaning:** at no time in the past and until now (negative from the past until now)

b. **Position in sentence:** between the auxiliary *have/has* and the verb

c. **Negative statements and questions:** We do not use *never* in negative statements or questions with present perfect verb forms. Be sure you do not make negative sentences with *never* as this will make two negatives.

> **Incorrect:** She hasn't never read some tall tales about Pecos Bill.

3. **Ever**

Have you ever studied tall tales in your classes?

a. **Meaning:** at any time (from the past until now)

b. **Position in sentence:** Use this adverb only in negative statements and questions with present perfect verbs. Do not use this adverb in positive statements.

> *Have you ever studied* about tall tales? *I haven't ever studied* about tall tales.*

> **Incorrect:** She has ever studied about tall tales.

4. **Yet**

Have you learned about Pecos Bill and Paul Bunyan *yet*?

a. **Meaning:** until now (from any time in the past to now)

b. **Position in sentence:** Use this adverb at the end of a sentence in negative statements and questions only. Do not use this adverb in positive statements.

> *Have you learned* about Pecos Bill *yet*? *We haven't learned* about him *yet*.

> **Incorrect:** We have learned about Pecos Bill yet.

---

*NOTE: When we use *ever* in negative sentences, we use a contraction.

Practice

Activity 1

Write the letter of the response on the right to each question or statement on the left. Use each answer only one time. Then circle all the present perfect verb forms and the adverbs from this lesson (never/ever/already/yet).

_____ 1. Have you ever heard of the Tales of 1,000 Nights?

_____ 2. Has your class finished Unit Six in the book yet?

_____ 3. I've never listened to tall tales about about Paul Bunyan.

_____ 4. Has your instructor already explained the project for this unit?

_____ 5. Why have you waited to write the paper about Pecos Bill?

a. Really? I've already gone to two storytelling sessions about him.

b. Yes, but I have never read those stories.

c. No, she hasn't ever mentioned that assignment.

d. I haven't found all the assigned stories yet.

e. No, we haven't completed the last part of it.

Activity 2

Rewrite each sentence below using the adverb in parentheses. Be sure to put the adverb in the correct position in the sentence. Follow the example.

1. (already) Have you spoken to the storyteller?

   Have you already spoken to the storyteller?

   OR   Have you spoken to the storyteller already?

2. (never) I have met her.

   _____

3. (yet) Has she arrived at the library?

   _____

4. (already) Yes, she has told a few stories.

   _____

5. (ever) Have you gone to a live storytelling session?

   _____

6. (ever) No, I haven't attended one in person, so I am excited to hear her.

   _____

Activity 3

A. *Fill in the blank spaces with the present perfect form of the verb in parentheses. Be sure to make the verb negative where indicated.*

B. *After you fill in the verbs, circle the correct adverb. In one case you should circle both adverbs because they are both possible.*

1. (review) _____Have_____ you _____reviewed_____ the fables for the

   quiz (already /(yet))?

   Yes, but I (be–*negative*) _____ able to understand all the

   morals (never / yet).

2. (take) _____ Bob (never / ever) _____ time

   to study creation stories from different cultures?

   (see) Yes, but he _____ (never / already) _____

   any information about stories from Native American cultures.

3. (find) _____ scientists (ever / already) _____

   evidence of truth to some of the very old legends and stories?

   (be) Yes, they have found some things, but nobody _____

   (ever / never) _____ able to prove the oldest stories.

4. (read) Some of the stories that I _____ say "anonymous."

   What does that mean?

   (identify) It means people _____ (already / never)

   _____ the original author.

 Activity 4

Find and correct seven mistakes in the following conversation.

Joe: How's school this semester? How has you liked the comparative
            literature class? Have you yet compared different creation
            stories?

Rebecca: No, we haven't get to those stories yet. We've studied already
            some flood stories and compared those, though.

Joe: We've already started some creation stories in my class, but we
            didn't made any comparisons yet.

Rebecca: Also, last week our instructor has explained some scientific evidence about large floods.

Joe: Do scientists really think that some places have experienced such large floods in reality ever? That sounds very interesting.

 Activity 5

Fill in the spaces with the present perfect form of one of the verbs on the list. Use each verb only one time. Then add the adverb in parentheses to the correct place in the sentence. Follow the example.

be	cover	learn	study	understand

A. Jim: (ever) _____Have_____ you _____ever studied_____
1   2
present perfect verb forms in your English classes?

Sharon: (already) Yes, we _____ that topic in our ESL
3
103 class. However, (never) I _____ it
4
completely.

Jim: I know. We _____ those verb forms twice in my
5
ESL classes, but (never) I _____ able to feel
6
comfortable using them in my writing.

be	go	hear	need	review	think

B. Sharon: We _____ the uses of the present verb forms
1
several times this semester, (yet) but I _____
2
very successful using them in my papers. I

_____ to continue to review them since the
3
teacher's last lesson.

Jim: I have an idea. Let's go to the Tutoring Center together at
school and get some extra help. I _____ good
4
things about that place from some friends. (already) They

_____ there and gotten help.
5

Sharon: I (already) _____ about getting some extra
6
help. Let's go!

Activity 6

A. *Answer each question either* yes *or* no. *If your answer is* yes, *write a sentence using* already. *If your answer is* no, *write a sentence using* ever *or* never. *Follow the examples.*

1. Have you ever been a storyteller?   Yes, I have already been a storyteller.

   No, I have never been a storyteller. OR No, I haven't ever been a storyteller.

2. Have you ever coped with a difficult situation in school?

   _____

3. Have you ever exaggerated a story when you told it?

   _____

4. Have you ever wanted to be like a fictitious character? (If yes, which one?)

   _____

5. Have you ever thought about a plot for an original story to write?

   _____

6. Have you ever listened to traditional oral tales from your culture?

   _____

7. Have you ever lived in a remote area?

   _____

8. Have you ever noticed a resemblance between your looks and someone famous?

   _____

B. *Share your answers with a partner. Then write some of your partner's answers. Be sure to use the adverbs* already, ever, *and* never *in each of your sentences. Follow the examples.*

EXAMPLES: Celia has already been a storyteller.

My partner has never been a storyteller. OR She hasn't ever been a storyteller.

_____

_____

_____

Present Perfect Progressive (Continuous)

From Past to Present with *For* and *Since*

Presentation

[1]People **have been telling** stories about the origins of the Earth and people **for thousands of years.** [2]These students **have been reading** some of those stories **since last week.** [3]The teacher **has been discussing** an assignment about these stories **since today's class started.**

Questions

1. What auxiliaries (helping verbs) do you see with the verbs in sentences 1 and 2? What auxiliaries (helping verbs) are in sentence 3?

2. What ending do you see on all the verbs in bold in these sentences? Write each of these verbs [without the auxiliaries (helping verbs)] on the lines:

   _____   _____   _____

3. What is the time in all of these sentences? How do you know this?

Explanation—Present Perfect Progressive with *For* and *Since*

1. In Lesson 35 you learned about using present perfect verbs for events or states that started in the past and continue to the present with *for* and *since*. Present perfect progressive (continuous) verbs also express time from past to present (unfinished) with *for* and *since*.

2. Present perfect progressive verb forms: have/has + been + verb + *-ing**

   $$\underset{1}{\text{have/has}} + \underset{2}{\text{been}} + \underset{3}{\text{verb}} + \underset{4}{\text{-ing}}^*$$

   People *have been telling* stories about the origins of the Earth and

   $$\underset{1}{\text{have}}\ \underset{2}{\text{been}}\ \underset{3}{\text{tell}}\underset{4}{\text{ing}}$$

   people for thousands of years.

   Be sure to have all four of these pieces, including the two auxiliaries (helping verbs) *(have/be)* and the *-ing* ending.

---

*See Unit 1, Lesson 6, page 35 for spelling changes with *-ing*.

3. **Negative sentences**

Follow the rule for making a sentence negative.

RULE: Add the word *not* after the auxiliary (helping verb) *have/has* to make a sentence negative. When there are two auxiliaries (helping verbs), place *not* after the first one.

People *have not (haven't)** been telling stories for thousands of years.

The teacher *has not (hasn't)** been discussing an assignment since the class started.

Follow this pattern for negative sentences using present perfect progressive verbs:

subject	first auxiliary *(have)* (helping verb)	not	auxiliary *(be)* (past participle)	verb + *-ing*	
People	have	not	been	telling	stories.
The teacher	has	not	been	discussing	an assignment.

4. **Questions**

   a. *Yes/No* **Questions**

   Follow the rule for making a question: Move the auxiliary (helping verb) to the left of the subject. When there are two auxiliaries (helping verbs), move the first one only.

   Have people *been telling* stories for thousands of years?

   Has the teacher *been discussing* an assignment since the class started?

   Follow this pattern for *yes/no* questions with present perfect progressive verbs:

auxiliary *(have)* (helping verb)	subject	auxiliary *(be)* (past participle)	verb + *-ing*	
Have	people	been	telling	stories?
Has	the teacher	been	discussing	an assignment?

   b. **Question word questions**

   Follow the rule for making a question: Add the question word and move the first auxiliary (helping verb) to the left of the subject.

   Why have people *been telling* stories for thousands of years?

   How long has the teacher *been discussing* an assignment?

---

*Contractions are often used in conversation. They are not usually used in formal writing.

Follow this pattern for question word questions with present perfect progressive verbs:

question word	first auxiliary *(have)* (helping verb)	subject	auxiliary *(be)* (past participle)	verb + *-ing*	
Why	have	people	been	telling	stories?
How long	has	the teacher	been	discussing	an assignment?

5. Use these verb forms for actions/events that started in the past, continue until now, and may continue into the future. These verbs often indicate duration (how long) of an event.

   Do not use these forms for non-action (stative) verbs. Use present perfect for non-action verbs. (See Lesson 8 to review these verbs.)

   Incorrect: People have been remembering these stories for thousands of years.

   Correct: People have remembered these stories for thousands of years.

6. Native speakers use the present perfect progressive forms for actions that started in the past and continue until now more often than the present perfect forms (unless the verb is non-action).

   There are a few verbs that we use in both the present perfect and present perfect progressive forms without a difference in meaning.

   These verbs include: live, work, teach, study, stay, wear

   We *have studied* legends and myths for two weeks.

   We *have been studying* legends and myths for two weeks.

7. Review of uses of present perfect and present perfect progressive:

Present Perfect	Present Perfect Progressive
• indefinite past or repeated past • action/state finished but no specific time	Not used
• from the past until now with *for/since* (not finished) • non-action (stative) verbs and sometimes other verbs	• from the past until now with *for/since* • shows duration (continuous/not finished) • not used with non-action (stative) verbs

Practice

Activity 1   (Review subordinating conjunctions of time in *Destinations 1 Writing for Academic Success*—Unit 6, pp. 155–166.)

Circle all the present perfect progressive verbs and put a line under for *and* since *and the words that follow them.*

1. My friends Heidi and Jason have been writing their own stories for three years.

2. Jason has been creating thrilling stories with fictitious heroes since he began writing.

3. He has been making new versions of these stories since last year.

4. Heidi has been revising all of her stories for a long time.

5. For the past two semesters, they both have been getting new ideas in their creative writing classes.

6. Their writing instructors have been helping them since they started taking the classes.

Activity 2   (Review subordinating conjunctions of time in *Destinations 1 Writing for Academic Success*—Unit 6, pp. 155–166.)

Fill in the spaces with the present perfect progressive form of the verb in parentheses. Be sure to make the sentence negative or a question if indicated. Then circle for *or* since. *Follow the example.*

> **EXAMPLE:** A literature class has a guest speaker today, and this person (speak) _____has been speaking_____ (for / (since)) the class started an hour ago.

1. The speaker (tell) _____ stories (for / since) an hour.

2. He (use) _____ his hands (for / since) he started his stories.

3. He (exaggerate) _____ the abilities of the heroes in his stories (for / since) the entire sixty minutes.

4. What (do) _____ the students _____
   (for / since) all this time?

5. Most of them (pay) _____ attention (for / since)
   the speaker began.

6. They (talk–*negative*) _____ to each other
   (for / since) the beginning.

7. Only a couple of the students (listen–*negative*)
   _____ (for / since) the last five minutes.

8. One student (take) _____ notes (for /since)
   about 20 minutes.

9. Some of them (expect) _____ the speaker to
   finish (for / since) three o'clock.

Activity 3

Find one mistake in each sentence and show how to correct each one.

1. Two students have be working on a difficult assignment for their class.

2. Gretchen has been going to the library every day for last week.

3. She has been look for more stories in books there.

4. She not has been finding enough information for her report.

5. Jose been searching for stories online since the class received
   the assignment.

6. He have been joining online discussions about Native American stories
   for the past week.

7. Both students have been wanting more help with this project since
   the teacher assigned it.

8. They has been discussing ideas for their project with friends since
   last weekend.

9. They have asking their friends for new ideas for several days.

10. One friend has been call them with several ideas since yesterday.

Activity 4

Read each statement below. Then decide if the second statement is true or false according to the meaning of the first one. Write T *for true or* F *for false on the line next to the sentence. Follow the example.*

1. People have been creating fictitious stories for thousands of years.

   __T__ People continue to tell these stories even today.

2. Sometimes a storyteller has tried to explain natural occurrences, such as thunder and lightning, through these stories.

   _____ Storytellers have already created some stories to explain natural occurrences.

3. People have been listening to these stories for many years.

   _____ People no longer listen to these stories.

4. In some cases, storytellers have been exaggerating their characters or making their stories more humorous through the years.

   _____ Storytellers continue to exaggerate characters and add humor to their stories.

5. In other cases, some stories have had changes to their plots or characters.

   _____ These changes took place already but we don't know exactly when.

6. For example, storytellers in Africa have been telling the Anansi spider stories for hundreds of years.

   _____ Storytellers in Africa no longer tell these stories.

7. Because slaves and others told these stories a bit differently, in some parts of the United States, Anansi has become Aunt Nancy.

   _____ These stories have already changed the character from Anansi to Aunt Nancy, but we don't know exactly when.

Activity 5

Fill in the spaces with either present perfect or present perfect progressive verb forms. If you think both forms might fit, use the present perfect progressive. One answer will be negative.

1. Many people in different cultures (explaining)

   _____ natural occurrences through different

   versions of the same story for thousands of years.

2. For example, a story about a great flood (circulate)

   _____ in many parts of the world for a very

   long time.

3. People (hear) _____ these flood stories

   many times in many societies.

4. In my literature class we (compare) _____

   stories about a great flood since the beginning of the semester.

5. Some scientific evidence of the reality of a great flood (get)

   _____ attention from many researchers.

6. In other words many people (believe)

   _____ these stories for so many years for

   good reason.

7. They (know) _____ that these stories

   (be–*negative*) _____ completely fictitious.

Activity 6

Write five sentences about what you have been doing in your classes since they started. Use for *or* since *in at least three sentences and be sure to use present perfect progressive verb forms in all of your sentences. Follow the example.*

In my English class we have been studying Unit Six since last week.

_____

_____

_____

_____

_____

_____

Appendix A

Irregular Verb List— Past Forms and Past Participle Forms

Base	Past	Past Participle
be	was/were	been
beat	beat	beaten
become	became	become
begin	began	begun
bet*	bet	bet
bite	bit	bitten
bleed	bled	bled
break	broke	broken
bring	brought	brought
build	built	built
buy	bought	bought
catch	caught	caught
choose	chose	chosen
come	came	come
cost*	cost	cost
cut*	cut	cut
dig	dug	dug
do	did	done
draw	drew	drawn
dream	dreamt (or dreamed)	dreamt (or dreamed)
drink	drank	drunk
drive	drove	driven
eat	ate	eaten
fall	fell	fallen
feed	fed	fed
feel	felt	felt
fight	fought	fought
find	found	found
fit*	fit	fit
fly	flew	flown
forget	forgot	forgotten
freeze	froze	frozen
get	got	gotten (British: got)
give	gave	given
go	went	gone
grow	grew	grown
hang (an object)	hung	hung
have	had	had
hear	heard	heard
hide	hid	hidden (or hid)

(continued)

* The verbs marked with an asterisk (*) have one form for the base, the past, and the past participle.

Base	Past	Past Participle
hit*	hit	hit
hold	held	held
hurt*	hurt	hurt
keep	kept	kept
know	knew	known
lay	laid	laid
leave	left	left
lend	lent	lent
let*	let	let
lie	lay	lain
light	lit	lit (or lighted)
lose	lost	lost
make	made	made
mean	meant	meant
meet	met	met
pay	paid	paid
put*	put	put
quit*	quit	quit
read*	read	read
ride	rode	ridden
ring	rang	rung
run	ran	run
say	said	said
see	saw	seen
sell	sold	sold
send	sent	sent
set*	set	set
shake	shook	shaken
shoot	shot	shot
show	showed	shown
shut*	shut	shut
sing	sang	sung
sit	sat	sat
sleep	slept	slept
speak	spoke	spoken
speed	sped	sped
stand	stood	stood
steal	stole	stolen
sweep	swept	swept
swim	swam	swum
swing	swung	swung
take	took	taken
teach	taught	taught
tear	tore	torn
tell	told	told
think	thought	thought
throw	threw	thrown
understand	understood	understood
upset*	upset	upset
wear	wore	worn
win	won	won
write	wrote	written

* The verbs marked with an asterisk (*) have one form for the base, the past, and the past participle.

Appendix B

Non-Action (Stative) Verbs

Emotions	Perceptions/Senses	Possession	Mental States
care	feel	belong	believe
dislike	hear	have	feel (believe/opinion)
doubt	see	own	forget
fear	smell	possess	imagine
hate	taste		know
like			mean
love			mind
mind			realize
please			recognize
regret			remember
respect			think (believe/opinion)
trust			understand

Wants/Needs/Preferences		Other	
hope		appear	look
need		be	owe
prefer		contain	seem
want		cost	sound
		equal	weigh

Appendix C

Pronouns

	Subject	Object	Reflexive	Possessive
SINGULAR				
• first person	I	me	myself	mine
• second person	you	you	yourself	yours
• third person	he/she/it	him/her/it	himself/herself/itself	his/hers
PLURAL				
• first person	we	us	ourselves	ours
• second person	you	you	yourselves	yours
• third person	they	them	themselves	theirs

Appendix D

Possessives

Possessive Nouns	Possessive Adjectives	Possessive Pronouns
1. noun + 's John's book 2. noun ending in *-s* Luis' job *OR* Luis's job 3. two people (owning the same thing) Luis and Marta's house.	my book your book his/her book/ its tail our book your book their book	It is mine. It is yours. It is hers/his. It is ours. It is yours. It is theirs.

Appendix E

Meanings of Modals and Equivalent Expressions

Meaning	Modal	Equivalent Expression(s)
ability	can could	be able to
requests	would could will can	
permission	could may can	
advice/suggestion	should	ought to had better (stronger)
necessity/obligation	must	have to
possibility	might may could	
probability (make a conclusion)	must	
predictions	will	be going to + verb
plans/intentions	will	be going to + verb
offers	will	
expectations		be going to + verb

Appendix F

Verbs Followed by Gerunds (verb + -ing)

advise	dislike	imagine	prevent
appreciate	enjoy	keep (continue)	prohibit
avoid	explain	mind (not like)	quit
celebrate	feel like	miss	recommend
consider	finish	postpone	suggest
delay	forgive	practice	understand
discuss	give up		

Appendix G

Verbs Followed by Infinitives (*to* + base/simple form of verb)

agree	fail	need	request
ask	grow	offer	seem
attempt	help	plan	wait
can't wait	hope	prepare	want
choose	hurry	promise	wish
decide	learn	refuse	would like
expect			

Appendix H

Verbs Followed by Object + Infinitive*

advise	force	pay	teach
allow	get	permit	tell
ask	help	promise	want
cause	hire	remind	warn
choose	invite	request	wish
encourage	need	require	would like
expect	order		

*Note that many of the words on this list also appear on the previous list. These words may be used with or without objects, depending on the context.

Appendix I

Verbs Followed by Either Gerunds or Infinitives

begin	continue	hate	love	remember	stop
can't stand	forget	like	prefer	start	try

Appendix J

Noun Spelling Changes—Spelling Rules for Nouns

Regular Plurals of Nouns

1. Add -*es:* nouns that already end in -*s* class/classes gas/gases

    nouns that end in -*ch, -sh, -x* or -*z* tax/taxes ash/ashes

    many nouns that end in -*o* hero/heroes tomato/tomatoes

2. Drop -*y* and add -*ies:* nouns that end in a consonant (*b, c, d, l, m, p,* etc.) followed by -*y*.
    city/cities story/stories

3. Drop -*fe* and add -*ves:* wife/wives life/lives

Irregular Plurals of Nouns

1. No -*s* ending:

man–men	mouse–mice
woman–women	foot–feet
child–children	goose–geese
person–people	tooth–teeth

2. No form change (same for singular and plural)

Chinese	antelope
Japanese	deer
Swiss	sheep
Vietnamese	shrimp

Appendix K

Grammar Glossary

adjective

An adjective describes something. It may come before a noun or after a linking verb.

She *is happy* today.
linking verb + adjective

I read an *interesting book* last night.
adjective + noun

Add *-er* or *-est* to an adjective, and it becomes a *comparative* or a *superlative* adjective.

She is *taller* than her sister.

Last night I ate the *biggest* piece of chocolate cake.

article

An article works with a noun. It tells us if something is specific or not specific, familiar or not familiar.

I ate *an* apple this morning.
not specific/not familiar

The apple was delicious.
specific/familiar

auxiliary (sometimes called helping verb)

An auxiliary or helping verb works with a verb. It usually comes before the main verb. An auxiliary often helps make negative statements and questions. There are two groups of auxiliaries,

1. *be*, have**, do***

   *Be is a special case. It can work with the verb as a helper, or it can be the main verb of a sentence.

   He *is* a hard worker.
   main verb (linking verb)

   He *is* tired today.
   main verb (linking verb)

   He *is working* late today.
   auxiliary + verb

   I *was working* at midnight last night.
   auxiliary + verb

   **Have and *do* can also be main verbs.

   I *have* a lot of homework to complete tonight.
   main verb

   We *have written* since last month.
   auxiliary + verb

   We always *do* our homework on time.
   main verb

   She *does* not *complete* her homework on time.
   auxiliary + not + verb

2. **modal auxiliaries:** *might, may, can, could, should, would, will, shall, must*

> He *can play* soccer today.   I *could* not *finish* my homework.
>
> *Will* you *go* there tomorrow?

clause

A clause is a group of words that contains a subject and a verb. Sometimes a clause is a complete sentence (independent clause), but sometimes it is not (dependent clause).

> I *ran* to the train station
> (independent clause-complete)
>
> If she *can* run to the train station
> (dependent clause-incomplete)

conjunction

A conjunction connects words and phrases as well as clauses.

> His father *and* mother live there.   I walked home, *but* she ran home.
>
> Do you want to go out *or* eat lunch at home?

object

An object receives the action of a verb. We usually place an object to the right of the verb.

> They wrote *letters* to their families.

gerund

Gerunds are words with an *-ing* ending, but they are not the verb of the sentence. Gerunds are the subject or object of a sentence. Gerunds follow certain verbs. (See Appendix F for this list.)

> *Studying* at the library *helps* me get good grades.
> gerund/subject   verb
>
> I *enjoy studying* at home in my room.
> verb   gerund/object

helping verb (See auxiliary)

infinitive

To + a verb is called an infinitive. We usually do not add any endings (such as *-s/-ed/-ing*) to infinitives.

An infinitive can be the object of a sentence. In this case the infinitive follows certain verbs. (See Appendices G and H for this list.)

> We *love to eat* at that restaurant.
> verb infinitive
>
> My friend *prefers to eat* at a different restaurant.
> verb infinitive

modal

A modal is a kind of auxiliary. It usually comes before the main verb. It is also used in questions and negative statements.

Modal auxiliaries: *might, may, can, could, should, would, will, shall, must*

She *should move* to a new apartment.
_{modal main verb}

She *may not want* to live there.
_{modal + *not* + main verb}

Could she *live* with us?
_{modal   main verb}

noun

A noun can be a person, place, thing, or idea. A noun can be *count* or *non-count*. Count nouns can be singular or plural.

I bought *a book* for my English class.
_{singular/count}

My friend bought *two books* for her class.
_{plural/ count}

The instructor gave a lot of *homework* to the class yesterday.
_{non-count}

preposition

A preposition shows a relationship between a noun or pronoun and the verb of the sentence. We do not use a preposition with a subject and an object of a sentence.

Dr. Soto taught his class *in* the lab *at* 6:00 o'clock last night.
_{subject   verb   object preposition preposition}
_{(place)   (time)}

pronoun

A pronoun takes the place of a noun. See Appendix C for lists of pronouns.

<u>Peter</u> loves <u>basketball</u>.   *<u>He</u>* plays *<u>it</u>* really well.

quantifier

A quantifier works with a noun to indicate *how much*. Indefinite quantifiers are not specific amounts. They work with both count and non-count nouns.

We had *several tests* last month.
_{quantifier + count noun}

I had *a great deal of trouble* with the last test.
_{quantifier   +   non-count noun}

subject

A subject is who or what a sentence is about. We usually place subjects to the left of a verb.

Their uncle lives in Florida.   *She* finished school at 3 p.m.

time expression/ time word

There are many words and expressions to indicate time. You may hear these words referred to as *adverbs*. Look for time expressions/words in a sentence when the verb may not give enough information about the time.

He is visiting his uncle in Los Angeles *today*, He is visiting his uncle in Los Angeles *next week*.

Example time words/expressions:

yesterday   *last week*   *tomorrow*   *every day*   *right now*

verb

A verb is a word that can change with the time. There are different kinds of verbs:

- **action verbs**

  He *walked* to school yesterday.

  He usually *takes* a bus to school.

- **non-action (stative) verbs**

  I *remembered* your friend from the party.

  She *understands* grammar very well in this class.

- **linking verbs**
  A linking verb is a verb that connects the subject to the words that describe it.

  Your friend *seems* tired.

  Some students *are* in the lab right now.

Index